THE NATIONAL ERECTORS' ASSOCIATION AND THE INTERNATIONAL ASSOCIATION OF BRIDGE AND STRUCTURAL IRONWORKERS

Luke Grant

ARNO & THE NEW YORK TIMES
NEW YORK   1971

Reprint Edition 1971 by Arno Press Inc.

Reprinted from a copy in
The State Historical Society of Wisconsin Library
LC# 72-156414
ISBN 0-405-02922-5

American Labor: From Conspiracy to Collective Bargaining—Series II
ISBN for complete set: 0-405-02910-1
See last pages of this volume for titles.

Manufactured in the United States of America

United States
Commission on Industrial Relations

The National Erectors' Association

AND

The International Association of Bridge and Structural Ironworkers

By
LUKE GRANT

WASHINGTON, D. C.
1915

BARNARD & MILLER PRINT, CHICAGO

CONTENTS.

CHAPTER I.

The International Association of Bridge and Structural
Ironworkers was organized at a convention held in Pittsburgh
February 4, 1896. Five local unions were represented—New
York, Buffalo, Boston, Pittsburgh and Chicago. Each local
union had three votes in the convention, which was composed
of thirteen delegates.

Formed at a period when the use of structural steel in buildings was being developed, the organization had no fixed prece-
dents to follow. The erection of structural steel was at that
time just assuming the position of a distinct trade. In some
of the larger cities of the country, a few steel buildings had
been erected in the late '80s and the early '90s, but the industry may be said to have been in its infancy at the time the
International Association was formed.

Local unions of bridgemen existed in some sections of the
country for a number of years previous to the appearance of
the first steel skyscraper. The bridgemen were more skilled
in the framing of timbers than in the erection of steel, but
as the use of steel as a substitute for wood became general,
the same workmen readily adapted themselves to the changed
character of the work and became "bridgemen" instead of
bridge carpenters, as they had once been classed.

From bridge building to construction work, with the appearance of the first steel building, was a natural step for the
bridgeman to take, and in Chicago, the birthplace of the modern steel building, the Bridge and Construction Men's Union
was formed in 1891. Because of its having been the pioneer,
the Chicago union became Local No. 1 when the International
Association was formed.

Probably due to the fact that the trade of a structural ironworker does not require as high a degree of skill as some other
building trades, the wages paid the ironworkers when they
first organized, were much lower than the wages paid to other

mechanics with whom they came in contact on a building. It was some years before the structural ironworker was recognized as a skilled mechanic by the more favored and better organized trades, and it required years of effort for the ironworkers to advance their wages to the level of other trades, or to a point commensurate with the hazardous character of the work they perform.

From the lowest paid trade on a building, the ironworkers through organization have advanced their wages in fifteen years well toward the top of the column of upwards of thirty unions in the building industry. The sharp advance in wages in the structural iron trade has been more marked than in most of the other trades in the building industry, for the reason that the ironworkers started from a lower point.

The following comparison of the wage scale of structural ironworkers for the years 1902 and 1914 in ten of the principal cities, shows an average increase of 21 cents an hour in the period:

City.	Cents per Hour.	
	1902.	1914.
Baltimore	43¾	56¼
Boston	40	56¼
Buffalo	45	62½
Chicago	50	68
Cleveland	47½	70
Kansas City	37½	65
Minneapolis	40	62½
New York	56¼	62½
San Francisco	37½	75
St. Louis	50	75

In a study of the character of the membership of the Bridgemen's Union, there are three factors to be taken into consideration: the comparatively small degree of skill required, the extremely hazardous nature of the employment, and the shifting character of the work, which necessitates being "on the road" much of the time.

That the work requires less skill than most of the other building trades, is shown by the fact that the period of apprenticeship is fixed at six months in some agreements between the ironworkers and their employers, while the maximum apprenticeship period found in any contracts is eighteen months.[1]

In some agreements the maximum age of an apprentice entering the trade is placed at twenty-five years, in other agreements it is thirty years, and in the Pittsburgh district the maximum age limit is thirty-five years. It will be seen that if the lowest age limit is taken, the structural ironworker apprentice may have reached the age of manhood before taking up the trade.

In most of the skilled trades where an apprenticeship of from three to five years is required, the apprentices are boys of eighteen years of age or under when they enter the trade. Some unions provide that apprentices shall not be over seventeen years of age, while frequently they begin their apprenticeship at sixteen years.[2]

Boys are then in that formative period in their lives when the precept and example of the journeymen with whom they associate, have an influence on their character. In the well organized trades, the apprentices are admitted to the union during their apprenticeship period, and while they are being taught a trade, they also are receiving lessons in self-government and discipline. Attending meetings of their trade union, they hear discussions on trade agreements and relations with employers in their particular craft, so that by the time they become journeymen, they are fairly well versed in matters pertaining to collective bargaining and joint trade agreements.

Owing to the heavy nature of the work of a structural ironworker, which requires strength more than skill, it may be impracticable to employ youths as apprentices, but it is true that the structural ironworker does not get the advantages in

1—In a national agreement between the Erectors' Association and the International Association, effective May 1, 1903, and expiring Jan. 1, 1905, the apprenticeship period is placed at six months. Agreements in New York, Philadelphia and Pittsburgh fix the period at eighteen months. In Chicago the agreements make no specific provisions for apprentices.

2—In agreements between the Carpenters' Union in Chicago and its employers the age limit for apprentices is seventeen years.

training of the average building trades workman, who started to learn his trade as a boy. The men who constitute largely the membership of the bridgemen's organization, are those who have tried other occupations and who have simply "drifted" into the structural iron trade, attracted by the high wages which it offers.

The second factor, the dangerous nature of the employment, is shown in the number of fatal accidents which constantly occur in the trade. For the fiscal year 1911-1912, as shown by the report of the secretary-treasurer of the International Association, 124 death claims were paid out of a total membership of 10,928. Of the 124 deaths occurring in the trade that year, 109 were due to accidents. This is 1 per cent of the total membership.

The figures are more striking if it is considered that out of a total of 124 deaths in the year, only 15 were due to natural causes. In other words, 87.9 per cent died as a result of accidents and 12.1 per cent from natural causes.[1]

The citizen on the street corner, who is fascinated as he watches an ironworker on the end of a narrow beam twenty or thirty stories up in the air, is apt to wonder that the accidents are not more numerous than they are. The trade does not look inviting to the man on the street. For that reason only men endowed with physical strength and daring take up the work. Facing danger daily develops in the ironworker a sort of desperate recklessness, that the workman in a less hazardous occupation does not understand.

In following his occupation as a bridge builder, which constitutes a large part of the ironworker's trade, the workman is compelled to be away from his home much of the time. Railroad bridges have to be built many times miles away from any habitation. The calling is one that hardly attracts the home-loving married man. As a result, the trade develops a class of roving and irresponsible workmen, more noted for strength and physical courage than for trained skill and intelligence.

1—Report of Secretary McClory to Indianapolis Convention 1913. The death rate from accidents furnished by Secretary Harry Jones.

When the modern steel building made its appearance, it was followed in the natural course of events by the large construction company, which took contracts for the erection of steel structures in all parts of the country. Workmen were sent by these companies from one city to another, so that the nomadic habits developed in the bridgemen were perpetuated in the structural ironworker. This condition does not exist to the same extent today that it did ten years ago, but it still exists.

The trade which a man follows has a powerful influence on his character. If his work is uncertain and occasional, it has a tendency to make him shiftless and irresponsible. If it is exceptionally dangerous, he is apt to be daring and reckless. If his calling requires him to travel, with only short intervals in any given place, he is not likely to develop in a high degree the social habits that tend to ideal citizenship. A man's mental attitude toward the world is, in no small degree, determined by his trade or calling, which creates his immediate environment.

Because of these things, which are a part of the structural iron industry and inseparable from it, the average ironworker is denied the opportunities for self-development that are enjoyed by the average skilled mechanic in other trades. These factors must be taken into account in seeking to understand and explain certain actions and the forces and motives that lie behind them.

Conditions in the structural iron trade have changed materially for the better in the last fifteen years. Steel construction is common in every large city, which means that efficient workmen can be found in every large center of industry. The necessity for traveling to find employment has been minimized, but not eliminated in the erection of buildings. In the erection of bridges, the conditions have not changed in that respect and crews of workmen must of necessity be sent from one point in the country to another where bridges are being built.

In describing the material from which the Bridgemen's Union had to draw its membership, and the influence which organization has had on the individuals, the business agent of one local union said: "The organization has made men of a lot of irresponsible bums. Most of us a few years ago didn't know what it meant to wear a white collar. We were only half civilized; just a lot of bums roaming around the country.

"But we are being educated and the union is doing it by raising wages and teaching us self-respect. The employers have changed, too. I remember when a bridgeman wearing a white collar couldn't get a job. The foreman would say he was a dude, who didn't know his trade. It's different now. If a man is well dressed when he is looking for work, the foreman will size him up and conclude that he is a decent fellow who doesn't drink, or he could not afford to dress so well. So a neat appearance is an advantage today, but it is only a few years since the blue shirt fellows had it all in their favor. It's been a hard fight, but the bridgeman today is a different fellow from the bridgeman of even ten years ago. The union has made mistakes. We realize that, but what could you expect of us? A lot of irresponsible bums can't be expected to be diplomats."[1]

If this description of the structural ironworker, given by one of them, is accurate, it can readily be understood why men of the Sam Parks stripe gained ascendency in the early days of the union. It may explain why strong-arm methods made such a strong appeal to the membership when the union encountered opposition. It may explain why even the conservative men in the union, realizing the benefits which organization had brought, might have been inclined to overlook the methods used, as long as results were obtained. It may explain the blind loyalty which the ironworker feels toward his union and why he rallies to its support with his money and fealty when he thinks its existence is threatened. It may explain why agents of the union, convicted of violations of law in seeking to further the union interests, are regarded as "martyrs" and not as "criminals" by the union ironworker.

1—Interview with W. C. Aiken, business agent Pittsburgh Local.

CHAPTER II.

THE NATIONAL ERECTORS' ASSOCIATION.

The National Erectors' Association, against which the Bridgemen's Union has waged a continuous fight since the spring of 1906, was organized March 3, 1903, in New York City. The name adopted at the time the organization was formed, was the National Association of Manufacturers and Erectors of Structural Steel and Iron Work. The shorter title was adopted early in 1906 at the time the Association launched its "open shop" campaign in the structural iron industry.

Any individual, firm or corporation, engaged wholly or in part in the erection of iron and steel bridges or buildings, is eligible to membership. The membership is restricted to such firms as pledge themselves to the open shop principle; this restriction having been imposed after the open shop campaign began.

For a number of years the Association had no written constitution or by-laws and its form of organization was exceedingly loose. It was formed mainly for the purpose of dealing with the International Association of Bridge and Structural Ironworkers in matters pertaining to wages and hours of labor. Its members carried on work throughout a large territory and it was deemed expedient to have a national agreement with the union.

The advantage in having such an agreement appeared to be that uniform hours of labor and working conditions could be established throughout the country and a wage scale fixed for each locality, according to local conditions. Such an agreement was entered into a few weeks after the organization was formed. (See Appendix, p. 158.)

At the initial meeting at which the Association was formed, there were fifty-four firms represented, including the largest fabricating and erecting concerns in the country. Soon after the New England employers withdrew for local business reasons, which left the membership at about forty firms. This membership with only a little variance has been maintained up to the present time.

On the expiration of the agreement with the union January 1, 1905, it was not renewed on a national basis. The reasons for this are not quite clear today, but it does not appear that either side made any special effort to maintain the national contract. The local unions at that time, as in fact they always had been, were strongly impregnated with the idea of having complete local autonomy within their respective jurisdictions and preferred to deal with their employers locally.

The companies also may have preferred to have local agreements, as this would give them an advantage in dealing with the union. In localities where the ironworkers were well organized, the companies could make local agreements, while in the absence of a national agreement, they would be free to employ such men as they chose in localities where the men were not strongly organized. As a matter of fact, that is what the companies did, and was the cause of the final rupture in contractual relations which led to the fight for the establishment and maintenance of the so-called open shop.

While the agreement was not renewed on a national basis in 1905, there was no indication that the firms composing the Erectors' Association meant at that time to discontinue their relations with the union. On the contrary, local agreements were signed for New York, Philadelphia and other cities which continued in force throughout the year 1905. In their main provisions these local agreements were as favorable to the union as had been the national agreement and more favorable than the agreement between the New York Local and the local contractors, many of whom were not members of the Erectors' Association.[1]

1—The agreement between the iron workers in New York and the local employers for the year 1905 provided that foremen should not be members of the union. The agreement between the same local and the Erectors' Association provided that there should be no restrictions in the employment of foremen "regardless of whether such foremen are members of the union or not." Article 13 in both agreements. See Appendix, pp. 162-171.

As will be shown in more detail hereafter, the policy of the Erectors' Association underwent a complete change in the spring of 1906. Conditions at that time appeared favorable for the inauguration of a policy that would break the power and influence of the union.

In the fall of 1905 the union had declared a strike against the American Bridge Company, by far the largest and most influential member of the Erectors' Association. The strike had been extended to firms holding sub-contracts from the American Bridge Company, which resulted in the New York Local of ironworkers being suspended from the Joint Arbitration Board and the plan of arbitration, at that time in force between the unions and the Building Trades Employers' Association.

On January 1, 1906, the ironworkers in New York struck for an increase in wages. This involved members of the Erectors' Association who had not hitherto been drawn into the strike against the American Bridge Company, so that the time appeared propitious to deal the structural ironworkers an effective blow, as they were outside the reach of assistance from the other unions in the building trades.

The Erectors' Association saw its opportunity to establish open shop conditions on a national scale. A constitution was adopted and the Association organized on a firmer footing than it had hitherto been. Up to that time the only purpose which held the members of the Association together was that of dealing with the union. This was a weak link compared with the purpose of crushing the power of that union, so that for the first time in its history the Erectors' Association became an aggressive force with a definite object in view.

The object in view is outlined in Article III of the short constitution adopted, which reads: "The object of this Association shall be the institution and maintenance of the open shop principle in the employment of labor in the erection of steel and iron bridges and buildings and other structural steel and iron work." (Constitution Erectors' Association, Appendix, p. 191.)

The government of the Erectors' Association is vested in an executive committee of nine members, which has power to levy assessments, hire and fix the salary of the Commissioner and other employees and to determine policies. The constitution contains eight brief articles dealing with membership, objects, government, dues and assessments and meetings. It has never been considered of sufficient importance to put in printed form. It provides that any of the articles may be amended by a three-fourths vote of the entire membership, except Article III quoted above. The inference is that the open shop article is fixed and immutable and cannot be changed while the Association lasts. (Constitution, Appendix, p. 191.)

The membership of the National Erectors' Association in September, 1914, was composed of the following thirty-three firms:

American Bridge Co.
Blodgett Construction Co.
Brann & Stuart Co.
Eastern Bridge & Structural Co.
John Eichleay Jr. Co.
Fay Hunt Erecting Co.
Fort Pitt Bridge Works.
Heyl & Patterson, Inc.
Illinois Steel Co.
Kansas City Bridge Co.
Levering & Garrigues Co.
Lucius Engineering Co.
McClintic-Marshall Construction Co.
Midland Bridge Co.
Million Bros. Co.
Missouri Valley Bridge & Iron Co.
New England Structural Co.
Pennsylvania Steel Co.
Phoenix Bridge Co.
Pittsburgh Construction Co.
Post & McCord.

Riter-Conley Manufacturing Co.
Roanoke Bridge Co. (Receivers.)
Seaboard Construction Co.
Lewis F. Shoemaker & Co.
Snare & Triest Co.
Terry & Tench Co., Inc.
Van Dorn Iron Works Co.
Virginia Bridge & Iron Co.
Wisconsin Bridge & Iron Co.
Western Steel Construction Co.
Worden-Allen Co.
Youngstown Construction Co.

During the first few years of the open shop campaign, the assessments paid by members of the Erectors' Association were based on the number of men each employed. Payment on a tonnage basis was later adopted. From these figures it is possible to arrive at a fairly accurate estimate of the extent of the open shop movement in the structural iron industry.

In the year 1908 the members of the Erectors' Association paid assessments on an average payroll of 3,512 men. The number for the first six months of the year was 3,810 and for the second six months, 3,214. For the first six months of the year 1909, up to the time the tonnage basis was adopted, the average number of men employed was 2,278. The falling off in the number of "open shop" men is accounted for partly by a business depression and partly by the fact that some firms failed to pay assessments within the period mentioned.

In the same years, 1908-9, the membership of the International Association of Bridge and Structural Ironworkers was 9,607. It will be seen, therefore, that the Erectors' Association was employing a force of about 36 per cent of the total union membership. The membership of the union that year was less than any year since 1905, but all the union members are not engaged in structural erection work. Nearly one-third of the total membership are ornamental ironworkers, who are not employed to any extent by members of the Erectors' Association. The union membership includes also machinery movers, piledrivers and some shop men, so that it may be said that about 45 per cent of the structural iron work done in that year, was conducted on the open shop plan. Of course a number of union men worked for members of the Erectors' Association, while on the other hand a number of firms, not members of the Erectors' Association, conducted their work on the open shop principle.

If the tonnage basis is taken the proportion of union and open shop work is approximately the same as shown by the number of men employed. In the year 1913 members of the Erectors' Association paid assessments on 948,000 tons fabricated and 430,000 tons erected in round numbers.

The following table taken from the books in the headquarters of the National Erectors' Association in New York, shows the tonnage on which each firm paid assessments for 1913:

APPROXIMATE TONNAGE FABRICATED AND ERECTED DURING 1913
BY MEMBERS OF THE

NATIONAL ERECTORS, ASSOCIATION.

	Fabricated.	Erected.
American Bridge Co.	606,771	132,183
Blodgett Const. Co.	.....	204
Brann & Stuart Co.	.....	2,585
Eastern Bdge. & Str. Co.	7,716	1,602
John Eichleay Jr. Co.	10,896	1,236
Fort Pitt Bridge Works	21,599	3,323
Heyl & Patterson, Inc.	2,679	2,373
Illinois Steel Co.	31,428	.....
Kansas City Bridge Co.	......	5,076
Levering & Garrigues Co.	19,750	13,879
McClintic-Marshall Const. Co.	99,054	62,562
Midland Bridge Co.	.....	1,500
Mo. Valley Bdge. & I. Co.	3,600	2,400
New England Struct. Co.	10,885	3,242

	Fabricated.	Erected.
Penna. Steel Co.	73,962	*36,981
Phoenix Bridge Co.	19,711	10,232
Pittsburgh Const. Co.	.....	27,458
Post & McCord	.....	44,543
Riter-Conley Mfg. Co.	.....	27,981
Roanoke Bridge Co., Inc.	3,768	372
Seaboard Const. Co.	.....	1,967
Lewis F. Shoemaker & Co.	11,688	4,161
Terry & Tench Co., Inc.	216	19,260
Western Steel Const. Co.	.....	4,927
Wisconsin Bridge & Iron Co.	16,376	9,782
Worden-Allen Co.	7,992	9,660
	947,091	429,489

The total tonnage of fabricated steel contracted for that year was approximately 1,300,000 tons.[1]

It will be seen, therefore, that on the basis on which they paid assessments, the members of the Erectors' Association erected 33 per cent of all the fabricated steel contracted for in the country in 1913, while they fabricated 73 per cent of the total.

It may be assumed that the members of the Erectors' Association do not pay assessments on more than their actual tonnage, so that if to the 33 per cent which they erected, is added the work done by independent firms under the open shop policy, the estimate of 45 per cent is a fair one.

This proportion of 55 per cent union and 45 per cent open shop steel construction, is not evenly distributed throughout the country. The open shop firms control practically all the bridge work, where there are no other unions to assist the

---

*—Estimated on basis of 50% of tonnage fabricated. The Penna. Steel Co. did not separate fabrication and erection tonnage in reporting to the Erectors' Association. It is probable that the actual figures for erection are considerably higher, as this company erects most of the steel it fabricates.

1—Figures supplied by Bridge Builders and Structural Society, New York.

ironworkers by sympathetic strikes. The union, on the other hand, controls practically all the building construction work in cities where the ironworkers are supported by other trades.

The stronghold of the Erectors' Association in building work is in New York City, where under the existing relations between the Building Trades Employers' Association and the building trades unions, the latter are not permitted to call strikes on any work being done by a member of the employers' association. The structural iron contractors in New York, whether members of the Erectors' Association or not, refuse to make any agreement with the Bridgemen's Union. This has been their policy since 1906, so that the entire trade in that city is on the open shop basis, although a few general contractors employ union ironworkers exclusively.

In Pittsburgh a somewhat similar situation prevails as to the preponderance of open shop work in the district. Figures furnished by the agent of the Erectors' Association in that city showed 1,033 open shop men working during the week ending September 26, 1914, in the Pittsburgh district, and 415 union men. The business agent of the union in a report made to the international headquarters for the same period, placed the number of open shop men at 1,000 and of the union men at 400, so that it will be seen both sides agree as to the proportion of union and open shop men.

It is throughout the eastern portion of the country that the open shop campaign of the Erectors' Association has been most effective. Its influence appears, however, to be gradually extending westward. The Erectors' Association recently opened offices in Kansas City. In Chicago the Association never has obtained a foothold in building construction work. The Bridgemen's Union in Chicago works under an agreement with the contractors and the same is true in most of the large cities in the Middle West and the West.

The Erectors' Association maintains district offices and employment bureaus in New York, Pittsburgh, Cleveland and Kansas City.

With this view before us of the two contending factors in

an industrial dispute which has attracted wide attention for nine years, it is necessary to revert to the conditions which obtained in the industry previous to the outbreak of hostilities and trace the history of the ironworkers and their employers, to show the causes leading up to the dispute.

CHAPTER III.

EARLY NEGOTIATIONS FOR TRADE AGREEMENT.

During the first few years of its existence, the International Association of Bridge and Structural Ironworkers appears to have lacked many of the characteristics common to international labor unions. It was largely an organization on paper, the separate local unions conducting their affairs as seemed best suited to meet local conditions, without regard to the international. There was little cohesion among the locals and no centralized form of government such as was later developed.

For the first few years the international officers received no fixed salaries and worked at their trade, attending to the affairs of the organization in their spare time. The headquarters of the international were in the home of the secretary, in the city from which he was elected. No journal was published by the union to keep the membership informed on matters of common interest, and the international did not affiliate with the American Federation of Labor until 1903, some eight years after it was organized.

In the year 1901 the organization began to function as an active national union and appears to have made rapid progress from that time. In July of that year the Bridgemen's Magazine appeared, and although conducted as a private enterprise until taken over by the international union in January, 1903, it appears to have had the effect of welding the different locals more closely, so that there was more unity of action among them.

At the convention of the international union in September, 1901, Frank Buchanan, a member of the Chicago Local, was elected president. He was not placed on a permanent salary, but he devoted a great deal of time in trying to put the organization on a firmer basis than it hitherto had been. He had broad ideas and realized that if the organization was to be made effective, united action on national lines would have to be taken, instead of individual action by separate locals.

As one of his first official actions, Mr. Buchanan sought a conference with Joshua Hatfield, president of the American Bridge Company, to discuss the question of making a national agreement. This conference, held November 25, 1901, resulted in arranging for another meeting, which was held at Pencoyd, Pa., on January 17-19, 1902. At this conference the American Bridge Company was represented by H. F. Lofland, erecting manager, and S. P. Mitchell, chief engineer. The international union was represented by Mr. Buchanan and D. F. McIntyre, at the time secretary-treasurer of the organization.

A tentative national agreement was reached, which appears to have been the best proposition that was ever offered the union by the American Bridge Company, or in fact by any of the large employing firms. In the proposed contract, the American Bridge Company agreed to employ only members of the union on all its erection work within the United States, and in territory outside the United States it agreed to give preference to members of the union.

The jurisdiction claims of the union, which at that time were causing some trouble with other unions, were fully recognized by the American Bridge Company and what appears more remarkable, Section 29 of the proposed contract provided that the union might engage in sympathetic strikes "to protect union principles" without such strikes being regarded as a violation of the contract.

This proposed agreement provided for a rather elaborate plan of arbitration for the settlement of differences that might arise over the interpretation of any clauses in the contract, or any other differences not specifically covered. Under it Boards of Referees were created in each of the three divisions into which the country was divided by the company, known as the Eastern, Pittsburgh and Western Divisions. Headquarters of these Divisions were in New York, Pittsburgh and Chicago.

The Boards of Referees were composed of two members,

one selected by each side in each division. When a dispute arose, if the two members could not adjust it, each selected another member, making a Board of four, two selected by the company and two by the union. If the full boards of four could not agree, provision was made for the selection of a fifth member, chosen by the other four, who could not be in any way connected with organized labor or the bridge building industry. A decision rendered by this independent umpire was final and binding on both parties, and such decision had to be made within six days from the date the fifth member was selected.

Another provision of the agreement provided that when the American Bridge Company sub-let a contract, the sub-contractor was subject to all the provisions of the original agreement. (Copy of Agreement, Appendix, pp. 149-158.)

In spite of the apparent advantages which the union would have gained by the acceptance of this proposed contract, it was rejected by all the large local unions in the country, with little or no consideration. The local officials of these unions today are at a loss to explain that seeming short-sightedness. Mr. Buchanan and the members of his Executive Board realized the importance of such a contract, as the American Bridge Company was by far the largest employer of structural ironworkers in the country and other large firms would in all probability have accepted the same agreement without protest. It would have resulted in completely organizing the trade, at a time when it was poorly organized outside a few of the larger cities. Mr. Buchanan and the Executive Board strongly recommended its acceptance.

In upbraiding an official of the New York local union of ironworkers some years later, for having rejected this proposed agreement Mr. Lofland said: "I worked for three days drafting the best agreement ever offered the ironworkers and your union didn't give it three minutes consideration."

This union official in relating the incident added: "And Mr. Lofland was right. We didn't give it one minute's consideration. Sam Parks arose and said we didn't want anything coming from Lofland and asked that it be thrown in the waste basket, which it was. We realize now what we threw away."[1]

It would appear that Mr. Buchanan's ideas were too far in advance of the membership of the local unions, which believed in purely local contracts and no interference from the international.

Although disappointed that the local unions did not accept the contract proposed, Mr. Buchanan continued his efforts to bring about national action to organize the trade. Early in 1902 when working at his trade on a building in Philadelphia, being erected by a Chicago firm, Mr. Buchanan learned that about one-half the structural iron work in Philadelphia was being done under non-union conditions. He planned to unionize some of the larger jobs by tying up the work of the same contractors in other cities.

In the furtherance of this campaign of organization, Mr. Buchanan caused strikes to be called in New York and Milwaukee on work being done by the same companies that were doing non-union work in Philadelphia.

At the same time, in 1902, the Philadelphia local called a strike against the American Bridge Company, which lasted from May 1 until August 13, and ended in a complete victory for the union. At the time the settlement was made the company had about 400 non-union ironworkers in its employ, most of whom had been imported from other cities. The settlement provided that all of those men who desired to join the union, should be permitted to do so and the rest should be discharged. About two-thirds of the number joined the union.

The success of the Philadelphia strike was due largely to the policy pursued by Mr. Buchanan and the membership of the union began to see the advantage of national action. All the large structural iron firms were doing an interstate business, so that it was generally possible to attack them at points where the union was strong and force them to unionize their work at points where the union was weak.

1—Statement of Charles Massey, Business Agent New York Local.

This policy, while causing some dissatisfaction among local unions, whose members could not see why they should be called upon to strike to assist another local, probably hundreds of miles distant, resulted in building up a fairly strong and effective organization.

At the convention of the International Association, held in Milwaukee in September, 1902, President Buchanan among other recommendations, urged that the president and secretary be placed on fixed salaries and devote their entire time to the work of the organization. He recommended that authority be given the president to adjust difficulties without waiting for the sanction of the Executive Board and that a contingent fund be set aside for the use of the president, so that he might proceed without delay to any part of the country where his services were needed. In other words, he urged the centralization of power and authority by vesting them in the hands of the chief executive officer.

Among the other recommendations made by President Buchanan were, a uniform road scale to govern wages and working conditions in territory outside the jurisdiction of established local unions; ownership and control of the Bridgemen's Magazine; establishment of an apprenticeship system and affiliation with the American Federation of Labor.[1]

The convention adopted all the recommendations, except that dealing with an apprenticeship system, which was laid over for one year to "permit the more thorough organization of the men in the craft."[2]

Following the convention a national road scale was adopted and put into effect, providing for a nine-hour workday and a minimum wage scale of $3.50 a day in all territory outside

1—Convention Proceedings, Bridgemen's Magazine, October, 1902.
2—No apprenticeship system has ever been adopted by the structural ironworkers' organization, although most of the local unions make some pretense of regulating the employment of apprentices. The Chicago local, which is the strongest numerically in the International Association, always has opposed apprentices and no provision for their employment is made in the agreements which the local makes with the employers,

the jurisdiction of local unions. This was the first uniform road scale adopted and it paved the way for a national agreement with the employers, an advantage that Mr. Buchanan did not lose sight of, in spite of his experience with the locals when he asked them to adopt the contract negotiated in the spring of 1902.

CHAPTER IV.

NATIONAL STRIKE AND NEW YORK LOCKOUT.

In the spring of 1903 the American Bridge Company was operating under signed agreements with the local unions of structural ironworkers in localities where circumstances made that expedient. In other localities where the ironworkers were not well organized, the company appears to have had little regard for union rules and regulations, so there was a good deal of friction.

In a report to the Kansas City convention of the international union in September, 1903, President Buchanan said that local unions in Buffalo, Pittsburgh, Philadelphia, Jersey City and Albany had "suffered grievances at the hands of the American Bridge Company, and that this company had been indifferent to the rights of these locals and had refused to adjust them."

The "grievances" complained of appear to have been of a more or less trivial character. No doubt they were aggravating to the local unions, and had they been allowed to go on without protest, it might have resulted in breaking down established standards, as other employers would have insisted on being granted like privileges.

Among the grievances enumerated by union officials active at that time were: the employment of more than one non-union foreman on a job; the holding back of a week's pay in making up payrolls, while the established custom was to hold back three days' pay; the working of three men on a riveting gang, while other firms used four men; the employment of laborers on false work that was claimed by bridgemen, etc.

In no instance has the claim been made that the American Bridge Co. paid lower wages to bridgemen than the rate agreed upon, nor did it require the men to work more hours, unless the employment of laborers at a lower rate of pay to do work claimed by skilled men, could be construed as a method of reducing wages.

The grievances enumerated were violations of established customs rather than of agreements, for in every written agreement found, there is a provision that there shall be no restriction as to the use of machinery, or any limitation of the work to be performed in a day. This provision is set forth in the first proposed national agreement, heretofore referred to as the most advantageous to the union which it had ever been offered. In fact, the provisions against restricting the use of machinery, or limiting the amount of work to be performed in a day, have always been accepted without question by the union, so that the employment of three men on a riveting gang instead of four, could hardly be termed a violation of the agreement.

In the only national agreement which ever existed between the American Bridge Company and the International Association is a clause which reads: ''There shall be no restriction as to the use of machinery or tools, or as to the number of men employed in the operation of the same.'' Another clause in the same agreement reads: ''There shall be no restriction whatever as to the employment of foremen.''[1]

It is quite evident, therefore, that the employment of three men on a riveting gang, or more than one non-union foreman on a job, was a violation of an established custom, but not of the letter of the written agreement. It is probable, however, that officers of local unions were more familiar with established customs and rules in their respective localities, than with the actual wording of the written contracts, and that when the American Bridge Company violated customs, it amounted in the minds of the union officials to a violation of agreements.

These differences, minor as they may appear on the surface, caused the Executive Board of the International Association to order a general strike against the American Bridge Company on March 12, 1903. It is possible that grievances of a more serious character, such as the employment of non-union men, existed in some localities, but the union officials dismiss

1—Copy of Agreement, Appendix, p. 160.

the subject with the general statement that there was "continual trouble" with the American Bridge Company and they cannot remember any specific details.

The general strike had been in effect about three weeks when President Buchanan secured an audience with the late J. Pierpont Morgan, at the latter's residence in New York. The meeting was arranged through the influence of officials of the National Civic Federation. Mr. Buchanan outlined the situation to Mr. Morgan in an hour's conversation, and the latter said that while he did not approve of the closed shop and some other features of unionism, he was in sympathy with organizations of labor in a general way and he would see what could be done in the matter.[1]

A few days later a conference was arranged between the officials of the American Bridge Company and other members of the Erectors' Association, which had been formed a week or two previously, and representatives of the union, and a national agreement was signed April 12, 1903, which became effective May first and continued in force until January 1, 1905.

This settlement, which was claimed as a complete victory by the union officials, may have had an important bearing on the attitude taken by the union some two years later, when another national strike was called against the American Bridge Company. The union felt that it was invincible, as it had scored a victory over the largest corporation in the country and what it had once done, it could do again.

Mr. Buchanan was greatly pleased at the signing of the national agreement. He personally did not think the contract was as good from the union standpoint as the one that the American Bridge Company had offered a year previously and which was rejected by the local unions, but it accomplished what he had been aiming at from the time he was elected president. It established contractual relations between the American Bridge Company and other large concerns and the iron-

1—Statement of Frank Buchanan, now a member of Congress.

workers on a national basis, and thus strengthened the position of the international union.

In a report to the following convention of the international union, President Buchanan in speaking of the agreement with the Erectors' Association, said: "This Association consisted of the principal structural iron manufacturers and erectors of this country and was by far the largest and most powerful of the associations of employers that had heretofore been formed.[1]

In actual wording this national agreement was an open shop contract, but in practice and effect it was strictly union or closed shop. The clause pertaining to employment read: "The employer may employ or discharge, through his representative, any workman as he may see fit, but no workman is to be discriminated against on account of his connection with a labor organization."

As the agreement was negotiated during the progress of a strike, it appears that provision was made to protect the men who had remained with the companies during the trouble, as one clause reads: "There shall be no discrimination against, interference with or fines imposed upon foremen who have been in the service of the employer during the time of strike."[2]

The agreement provided that in case of misunderstandings or disputes arising, the questions at issue should be submitted to arbitration locally, without strikes, lockouts or cessation of work. No provision was made as to how such local arbitration boards should be organized, as was the case in the more elaborate form of agreement rejected by the union the previous year. Neither was any provision made that subcontractors taking work from a member of the Erectors' Association should be subject to the terms of the original contract. The agreement provided that there should be no sympathetic strikes on account of trade disputes.

An eight-hour workday was fixed for all localities where it was the prevailing custom to work eight hours, and in other

1—President's Report to Convention, Bridgemen's Magazine, October, 1903.
2—Copy of Agreement, Appendix, p. 160.

places a nine-hour workday was the rule. The contract provided that the latter provision "may be subject to arbitration."

No minimum wage rate was established in the national agreement, but in each city or locality, a separate clause was added, specifying the rate of pay and the territorial jurisdiction granted to the particular local union.

That the Erectors' Association and the union worked in harmony, following the signing of the national agreement, is shown by various records. A conference was held July 14, 1903, between H. H. McClintic, H. A. Greene and J. F. McCain, representing the Erectors' Association, and Thomas Graves, J. E. McClory and J. M. Stark, representing the Cleveland local, to decide on territorial jurisdiction in Ohio. The following jurisdiction was agreed upon:

Cleveland ....radius of 25 miles from City Hall.
Columbus ....radius of 20 miles from City Hall.
Youngstown ....radius of 25 miles from City Hall.
Canton—City Limits.
Canal Dover, City Limits.
Ashtabula, including Erie, Pa., radius of 12 miles.

In the prescribed area the agreement provided for an eight-hour workday and a minimum rate of 50 cents an hour. In all other territory a nine-hour workday prevailed.[1]

A similar agreement was signed in Philadelphia by H. F. Lofland for the American Bridge Company and M. J. Cunnane for the union, establishing the wages at 50 cents an hour and the jurisdiction of the Philadelphia local to a territory within a radius of 50 miles from the City Hall of Philadelphia.[2]

Both sides to this contract agree that whatever the literal wording was, or the construction that might be placed on certain clauses, it was in practice a strictly union agreement and no complaint was made that the companies sought to violate this understanding by employing any ironworkers not members of the union. It also was the custom, established through

1—Bridgemen's Magazine, August, 1903.
2—Copy of Agreement, Appendix, p. 161.

a verbal agreement, that sub-contractors should be subject to the terms of the agreement, in the same manner as the original signers.

The national agreement seems to have been generally observed by both parties during its life and no serious difficulties arose in the trade, except in New York City, where the building contractors in 1903 adopted what became known as the Arbitration Plan and locked out the unions that refused to accept it. The structural ironworkers' union was one of those that balked at the Arbitration Plan and was locked out and a dual union of ironworkers formed by the employers. A few of the New York employers were members of the Erectors' Association, but they held membership also in the local association of iron and steel erectors, and it was as members of the local association that they made the fight. The New York lockout was a purely local affair and was not regarded by the union men themselves as a violation of the national agreement with the Erectors' Association. In fact Mr. Buchanan was in sympathy with the fight the New York employers were making against the union, which at the time was controlled by Sam Parks, with whose methods Buchanan did not agree.

This issue between the New York local and the International Association was fought out on the floor of the international convention, held in Kansas City in September, 1903. Mr. Buchanan won in his fight against the Parks faction and following the convention an effort was made to bring about a settlement of the New York lockout. Parks previously had been convicted in the courts of extortion and had regained his liberty shortly before the convention, pending hearing on a motion for a new trial. The new trial being denied, Parks was again committed to the penitentiary and many of the ironworkers in New York were demanding a new deal and a settlement with their employers.

A meeting of the International Executive Board was held in New York November 6, 1903, at which a proposed agreement was drawn up and submitted to the employers, who were members of the Building Trades Employers' Association. It was rejected by the employers, who submitted a counter proposition to the effect that the ironworkers accept the national agreement then in force with the Erectors' Association, with the exception of the arbitration clause. As a substitute for that clause the New York employers proposed to insert in the contract the arbitration plan of the Building Trades Employer's Association, which by that time practically all the building trades had accepted.

Mr. Buchanan and his Executive Board accepted the proposition and the question then arose as to the disposition of the dual union which had been formed by the employers and chartered under the state laws. The employers wanted to have the dual union chartered by the International and made the regular organization.

This proposition was rejected by the union representatives, but they offered to take into the union without any penalty such of the old members as had left and joined the dual organization, and also take in such other members as could pass an examination and prove their competency. The employers replied to that proposition, that their foremen would determine the question of competency. The union representatives then offered to allow the employers to select three of their foremen who with three members of the Executive Board would form an examining board and agreed that apprentice cards would be furnished to those who failed to qualify as journeymen.

The employers rejected this offer, as they were determined to break up the old Local No. 2, so long controlled by Sam Parks, and "scatter the clique" as one of them expressed it. The negotiations were broken off temporarily and the fight in New York continued.[1]

About three months later, in February, 1904, a settlement was made of the New York trouble, through the disbanding of old Local No. 2 and the formation of four new locals in

1—Report of President Buchanan, Bridgemen's Magazine, December, 1903.

the district, two in New York, one in Brooklyn and one in Jersey City. All the ironworkers in the district, union and independent, were required to register and pay a registration fee of 50 cents and all were accepted in the new locals without discrimination.

The agreement granted full recognition to the locals and provided for the employment of union men exclusively. The structural ironworkers became a part of the General Arbitration Board and the New York district became again thoroughly organized.

CHAPTER V.

Causes Which Led to Second National Strike.

Throughout the year 1904 the structural ironworkers made steady progress, with no serious difficulty anywhere, after the settlement of the New York dispute. In that year and the year following, the organization reached the highest point it had ever attained with respect to membership and influence.

As noted previously, there does not appear to have been any serious effort made by either side to have the national agreement renewed, on its expiration January 1, 1905. Officers of local unions in some instances sought to have the American Bridge Company renew the contract in their respective localities. In Philadelphia, Mr. Cunnane, the local business agent, obtained an interview with Mr. Lofland of the American Bridge Company, and on behalf of the local union he offered to accept the old agreement for one, two or five years. Mr. Lofland refused to sign.

At the time the American Bridge Company was building a bridge over the Schuylkill River for the Philadelphia Rapid Transit Company and on the afternoon of December 31, 1904, all the ironworkers were laid off. Officials of the company said they feared ice in the river might damage the false work.

Mr. Cunnane says he made a personal inspection of conditions in the river and there was no indication of ice for a distance of twenty miles up the stream. He asserts the purpose of the company closing down in the middle of winter was to compel the ironworkers to accept a less favorable contract than the one just expired.

Some three weeks later a local agreement was signed with the American Bridge Company, which Mr. Cunnane says was less favorable to the union than the old contract. It seems probable, however, that the differences between the new local contract, and the old national one, were exaggerated in the mind of Cunnane, for a reading and comparison of the agreements do not show any important difference. The agreement made with the Philadelphia local, except for a difference in the wage scale, was the same as that made with the New York district, which as already pointed out, was more favorable to the union than the one made with the local association of erectors in New York.

In the spring of 1905 it appears to have been the policy of the Erectors' Association and the American Bridge Company to sign agreements with the local unions in large cities like New York, Philadelphia and Boston and to ignore the locals in smaller cities. In February, 1905, the secretary of the New Haven local sent a copy of a proposed agreement to the Erectors' Association and in reply received a letter which read: "I wish to advise that the articles of this agreement are entirely unsatisfactory to us and under no circumstances will we agree to such conditions."[1]

Another letter was sent by the local union, to which no reply was made and it was this action which later led to the strike against the American Bridge Company.

The New Haven local, according to the statement of the secretary, was not in a position to enforce any demands in February and matters were allowed to drift until the following July, when the American Bridge Company sub-let the erection of a railroad bridge to the Boston Bridge Company, a non-union concern.

In the absence of a national agreement, or any contract with the New Haven local, the American Bridge Company was, of course, within its rights in sub-letting work to a non-union concern. In fact, in the cities where local agreements existed between the American Bridge Company and the ironworkers, no provision was made in such contracts that work should be sub-let only to union firms. There was a verbal understanding to that effect and it was the practice to observe it. The New Haven local was equally within its rights to declare a strike against the American Bridge Company in its jurisdiction, as it had no agreement, oral or written.

1—Statement of E. L. Warden, Bridgemen's Magazine, September, 1905.

The strike against the American Bridge Company was called by the New Haven local July 28, 1905, in an effort to force the company to sign an agreement and also to unionize the sub-contract let to the Boston Bridge Company.

That this strike had the approval of President Buchanan is shown by a letter which he wrote to Secretary McNamara from New York under date of July 28, 1905, setting forth the facts in the situation and requesting that the question of calling a national strike in support of the New Haven local be submitted to a vote of the Executive Board.[1]

After the members of the Executive Board had voted in favor of a national strike, Secretary McNamara issued from headquarters in Cleveland, "Circular No. 30 To Local Unions." In this circular it is stated that since the expiration of the national agreement, the American Bridge Company had shown marked discrimination against the New Haven local. The circular in part read: "No local union should ever allow any work to proceed under the subterfuge that it has been taken away from the American Bridge Company, as in the majority of cases this is but a move to outwit local unions."[2]

The national strike was ordered August 10, but it does not appear that the order was generally obeyed, owing, probably, to the fact that the convention of the international union was to be held early in September and also owing to the difficulty in determining what contracts had been sub-let by the American Bridge Company.

Contractors who had taken work under sub-contracts from the American Bridge Company, frequently denied that they had done so. In other instances the local unions refused to enter the fight, or call strikes on work that was being done under union conditions.

This was the situation at the time the international convention opened in Philadelphia in September. President Buch-

---

1—Exhibit No. 2, p. 1102, Vol. 2 Trans. of Record U. S. Court of Appeals.
2—Exhibit No. 4, p. 1098-9, Vol. 2 Trans. of Record U. S. Circuit Court of Appeals Dynamite Conspiracy Trials.

anan, who at the two previous conventions, had been re-elected by narrow margins, refused to be a candidate for re-election. His retirement, which seems to have been singularly unfortunate for the union at that particular time, was practically forced, according to some of the delegates to the convention. Mr. Buchanan believed he could have been re-elected had he wished to be a candidate.[1]

At the convention Frank M. Ryan, a member of the Chicago local, was elected president to succeed Mr. Buchanan and as there was a good deal of ill-feeling existed between the two, it is probable that the personal equation was an important factor in the events which followed.

The convention indorsed the strike against the American Bridge Company, by the adoption of a resolution which was the cause of the failure of future peace negotiations, because it practically tied the hands of the executive officers.

The resolution adopted by the convention was as follows:

"Resolved: That the delegates to the ninth annual convention of the Bridge and Structural Ironworkers do endorse the action of our late International President and the Executive Board in trying to preserve the unity and solidarity of our association, and we further instruct our incoming President and Executive Board to do everything they can to fight these

---

1—Mr. Buchanan held a small amount of stock in the McCain Construction Company, which at the time of the convention was fighting the union. The stock was purchased at a time when the company was fair and when Mr. Buchanan intended to retire as a union official and go into business. Later when the company was declared unfair, he could not dispose of his stock except at a sacrifice. Some of the delegates learned of the stock transaction, and according to the stories, threatened to bring the matter out on the floor of the convention, unless Mr. Buchanan agreed to retire. Mr. Buchanan never denied the ownership of stock in the company and considered it a straight business transaction. The incident is mentioned chiefly because of the credence given in certain quarters to stories reflecting on the integrity of Mr. Buchanan. Whatever may be said of the impropriety of a union official holding stock in a company which he might be called upon to fight in an official capacity, there is no evidence of any dishonesty in the transaction. Mr. Buchanan afterward disposed of the stock at a financial loss.

companies in their efforts to disrupt our association and not to call this strike off until every existing grievance is settled satisfactory to all our affiliated locals."[1]

Some time previous to the convention a strike had been called against the Pennsylvania Steel Company, for employing a repair gang to build an ore trestle within its plant at Steelton, Pa. The strike had been called by a local business agent against the direction of President Buchanan. The claim of the company was that the work in question did not come under the jurisdiction of the structural ironworkers.

This dispute was submitted to arbitration, the arbitrators being John W. Hutchinson, Jr., for the company and John T. Taggart, a member of the New York local for the ironworkers. The two arbitrators reached a decision without having to select a third man.

The finding of the arbitrators in substance was that the work in question was "bridge work" as commonly understood, but that the relations between the Pennsylvania Steel Company and the union applied exclusively to the bridge and construction department, and that the union hereafter refrain from claiming on behalf of its members any work in connection with departments of the company, other than the bridge and construction department.

A provision was made in the award which read: "Provided that if at any future time it shall become the general custom of steel works throughout the country to employ men who are substantially members of the Association in the erection of structural steel and iron for their own use, then the Pennsylvania Steel Company will do likewise."[2]

This finding was made about the time of the Philadelphia convention, with the approval of President Buchanan, but does not appear to have been announced until some time later. The finding waived the claims of the union to work done by steel companies for their own use, until that had become the general

---

1—Convention Proceedings, Bridgemen's Magazine, October, 1905.
2—Bridgemen's Magazine, November, 1905.

custom. The Illinois Steel Company at its South Chicago and Joliet plants, was the only company of importance in the country which was at that time employing union structural iron-workers in doing work around its plants.

This decision is of especial significance for the reason that it was an exactly similar case which caused the break in the peace negotiations at a conference held between the union representatives and officials of the American Bridge Company in October, 1905, when the union men would not waive their claim to the work of building a tube mill at the McKeesport plant of the National Tube Company.

Although this arbitration award was accepted by the union, so far as the particular job for the Pennsylvania Steel Company was concerned, it was severely criticised by some of the officials. Among the most severe critics was the newly elected president, Mr. Ryan, who blamed his predecessor in office for approving of the award.

CHAPTER VI.

Efforts to Reach a Settlement.

Following adjournment of the Philadelphia convention, President Ryan and the Executive Board held a conference in Philadelphia with S. P. Mitchell, chief engineer of the American Bridge Company, to discuss terms of settlement of the strike. Mr. Mitchell offered to employ union ironworkers on all erection work done directly by the company, but would not agree to sign any written contract to that effect. Neither would he give any guarantee that work sub-let by the company would be done by union men.

Mr. Ryan and his Executive Board insisted upon having a written contract and presented a draft of an agreement which they had drawn up. Mr. Mitchell asked for further time to consider the matter and take it up with the higher officials of the company. He agreed to meet the union representatives again within three weeks.

Mr. August Ziesing was made president of the American Bridge Company about September 1, 1905, a week or two previous to the time Mr. Ryan was elected president of the International Association of Bridge and Structural Ironworkers. The election of Mr. Ryan greatly pleased Mr. Ziesing, as he had known Ryan for some years in Chicago and entertained a rather high opinion of him. Accordingly Mr. Ziesing wrote Mr. Ryan a letter, requesting him not to call any more strikes against the company until an effort was made to reach a settlement. Mr. Ziesing said he would be going to New York in the near future and would be pleased to have a conference with the union officials.

Mr. Ziesing says he received no reply to his letter and that his request was ignored, as Mr. Ryan immediately proceeded to call strikes on all work which there was reason to believe had been sub-let by the company to firms employing union men.

In pursuance of the policy of extending the strike as rapidly as possible, Mr. Ryan proceeded to Chicago after the conference with Mr. Mitchell and Secretary McNamara went to Cleveland.

In Chicago Mr. Ryan urged that the men employed by the Illinois Steel Company be called out and that the work being done by the Kelly-Atkinson Company also be stopped. The latter named firm was supposed to have taken a sub-contract from the American Bridge Company, while the Illinois Steel Company was a subsidiary of the U. S. Steel Corporation, as was the American Bridge Company.

Some of the leaders in the Chicago local opposed the program urged by Mr. Ryan. Among them was Mr. Buchanan, Mr. Ryan's predecessor in office, who said the strike could be settled amicably and that while negotiations for a settlement were pending, it would be folly to call out more men. Mr. Ryan made an appeal to the union and won his point and the strikes were called.

Meanwhile the Cleveland local had refused to call its members off some jobs supposed to have been sub-let by the American Bridge Company and Secretary McNamara caused the union to be suspended. The fight was being pushed both by Mr. Ryan and Mr. McNamara as vigorously as they could, in spite of the fact that negotiations between the union and the company had not been broken off and that Mr. Ziesing had requested that matters be left in statu quo until he had an opportunity to confer with the union representatives.

On leaving Chicago Mr. Ryan went to headquarters in Cleveland and while there was informed that the officials of the U. S. Steel Corporation desired a conference. Accompanied by Secretary McNamara he immediately went to New York and was joined by Ben Moore, a member of the Executive Board.

The first conference was held in Mr. Ziesing's office. Mr. Ryan pointed out that the company was employing non-union men on a number of jobs, either directly or through sub-contractors. He mentioned the job in New Haven, which was the direct cause of the strike, a bridge job in Arkansas and two bridge jobs in Illinois for the McKinley Traction System. The erection of the McKeesport tube mill also was brought up.

Mr. Ziesing said he had no supervision over such work as the erection of the tube mill and suggested that the conferees go and see W. P. Corey, president of the U. S. Steel Corporation. Mr. Ziesing and the committee went accordingly to Mr. Corey's office.

No record appears to have been kept of the discussion which followed and Mr. Ryan and Mr. Ziesing do not quite agree as to the facts. E. H. Gary, chairman of the Board of Directors, was called into the conference, but his recollection of what transpired is hazy. He was called in as a mediator and his attitude throughout was conciliatory. That is Mr. Gary's own statement and it is substantiated by Mr. Ziesing and Mr. Ryan.

There were present at the second conference Mr. Gary, Mr. Corey, Mr. Ziesing and Mr. Mitchell for the company and Mr. Ryan, Mr. McNamara and Mr. Moore for the union.

Mr. Corey in opening the discussion said that the form of agreement presented by the union representatives was dishonest and a most extraordinary proposition, as it required the company to see that union men were employed on all sub-contract work let by it. After Mr. Ryan explained that such agreements were in effect in many localities and that the American Bridge Company itself had accepted the practice through a verbal understanding, Mr. Corey appeared to be considerably mollified and indicated that he did not see serious objection to the agreement.

When the McKeesport job was mentioned Mr. Corey said he would not agree to unionize that work and asked Mr. Ryan if the union meant to claim all repair work in the steel plants. Ryan replied that he was not making any such claim and pointed out that the Illinois Steel Company had always employed union structural ironworkers on new construction work in its plants.

Mr. Corey inquired of Mr. Mitchell how many men were employed on the tube mill at McKeesport and on being informed that there were about forty men, he remarked that the situation was not as important as he had supposed. After some further discussion, Mr. Corey advised the union representatives to confer with Mr. Ziesing and try to have all the other details settled and return later to take up with him the McKeesport job.

The conference was resumed in Mr. Ziesing's office and an understanding was reached on all the points in dispute, except the erection of false work and the employment of laborers in handling material on the site of the job. These points finally were left in abeyance to be taken up when a new contract was being formulated at the beginning of the next year.

These minor details having been adjusted the union representatives returned to Mr. Corey's office and informed him that everything had been settled except the McKeesport job and the question of having a written agreement. Mr. Corey conferred with Mr. Mitchell in another room and returned and informed the union representatives that he would not change his position on the McKeesport job. On the question of a written agreement, the company would not sign any contract embodying all the union rules, but did offer to reduce to writing what it had agreed to do, that is, employ only union men on all work done by it directly or by sub-contract; pay the recognized rate of wages and work the recognized number of hours.

When Mr. Corey refused to unionize the McKeesport job, Mr. Ryan said he could not make a settlement, as his instructions from the convention were emphatic on that point. The conference adjourned without a settlement.

That is substantially Mr. Ryan's version of what took place in the several conferences held and the cause of the final breakdown of contractual relations between the American Bridge Company and the union.

Mr. Ziesing says the union representatives demanded that the company should not sell steel to any concern employing nonunion men and that Mr. Gary pointed out that such an arrangement would amount to conspiracy and could not be considered.

During the discussion when the union representatives were

insisting on having a written agreement, Mr. Gary remarked that he did not see why that was essential, as Mr. Corey being present and agreeing to certain conditions, would see that Mr. Ziesing and Mr. Mitchell lived up to the terms agreed upon.

"We won't take your word for anything and want your signatures in black and white," is said by Mr. Ziesing to have been the reply of one of the union officials. Mr. Ziesing says he recalls distinctly that one of the union men brought his fist down on the table and said emphatically, "You'll sign up an agreement or we won't settle. Your word doesn't go with us," or words to that effect.

One of the union officials, according to Mr. Ziesing, said during the discussion that the union would organize the shops of the company by refusing to handle material manufactured by non-union men and after that was accomplished the shop men would refuse to handle steel rolled in non-union mills. Mr. Ryan says that the question of shop work was not an issue in the strike, consequently there could have been no purpose in raising it during the discussion and that Mr. Ziesing's memory is at fault on that point. Mr. Ryan thinks, however, that Mr. Mitchell may have pointed out such possibilities to Mr. Corey and Mr. Ziesing to prevent them making a settlement with the union, as Mr. Mitchell showed by his attitude that he did not want a settlement.

In recalling to memory the discussion during the conferences, Mr. Ziesing says three points stand out prominently in his mind today. These points are the demand on the company not to sell steel to non-union firms, the threat of organizing the fabricating shops and a demand that the union steward on a job should decide on whether a workman could be discharged. He thinks the McKeesport job was only incidental, as it had always been the practice of steel companies to use their own repair gangs on such work.

After Mr. Corey had given his final word on the McKeesport job, Mr. Ziesing says that he urged Mr. Ryan to accept the compromise offered, saying: "It is your last chance, Ryan. If you do not accept this proposition now, you will never have another opportunity as long as I am president of the company."

"Oh, hell, you may not be president long," is the reply which Mr. Ziesing says Mr. Ryan made to him.

After the conference with the steel officials ended without a settlement having been reached, the union officials held a conference by themselves in a hotel. The local union officers attended this conference and Charles Massey, business agent of the New York local, urged the acceptance of the compromise. The New York structural ironworkers were preparing to demand a wage increase on the expiration of their agreement two and a half months later and Mr. Massey was anxious to avoid trouble over the national issue. At that time the New York local had not been drawn into the controversy.

Mr. Ryan went to Pittsburgh and appeared before that local to urge that it waive claim to the erection of the tube mill at McKeesport, so that a settlement could be reached. He personally favored acceptance of the offer made by the company.

The Pittsburgh local refused to consider the suggestion. Some of the more radical members demanded to know if they were being "sold out" or why their international president was making such a proposition to them, in face of the action taken by the recent convention. The result was that Mr. Ryan left Pittsburgh resolved to keep up the fight.

CHAPTER VII.

REASONS WHY PEACE CONFERENCE FAILED.

In looking for the direct causes for the breakdown of contractual relations between the American Bridge Company and the International Association of Bridge and Structural Ironworkers, there are two main factors to be considered. These are, first, the well established policy of the U. S. Steel Corporation to maintain the open shop and prevent the spread of unionism in any of its departments, and second, the tendency of the structural ironworkers, in common with all other organizations of labor, to extend their sphere of activity and influence.

There were contributory causes, such as questions of policy, personal ambition, mutual distrust, love of power, lack of diplomacy, etc., but they were subordinate to and grew out of the two main causes.

The policy of the U. S. Steel Corporation at the time of its formation and for several years thereafter, was to prevent the spread of organization among its employees, rather than to crush existing organizations. This policy, pursued to its logical conclusion, would in the end have the effect of crushing the unions, but the process would be gradual and attract less public attention than an open fight resulting in strikes or lockouts.

That this was the policy of the corporation in the beginning, is shown by the strike of the Amalgamated Association of Iron, Steel and Tin Workers in 1901. The strike of the steel workers took place a few weeks after the U. S. Steel Corporation was formed. Before the strike was called, the representatives of the subsidiary companies, offered to renew all existing contracts with the union. In other words, the offer was made to sign up for all mills which had been signed for the previous year, but not to include non-union mills which had been absorbed in the combination.

This partial signing up of mills was not satisfactory to the leaders of the Amalgamated Association. They feared the purpose of the corporation was to close down and dismantle some of the mills that had been union and transfer the business to non-union mills.

There are good reasons to believe that that was in fact what the corporation intended to do. Whatever the intentions of the corporation were, the steel workers went on strike and were defeated, being forced at the end of three months' strife to accept a settlement for a smaller number of mills than they could have obtained without a strike.

Early in September, 1901, after the strike had been in force about three months, the corporation at a conference in New York, brought about by representatives of the National Civic Federation, offered to sign an agreement for 18 out of 24 tin-plate mills, 14 out of 24 sheet steel mills and 7 out of 13 steel hoop mills. Acceptance of this offer was strongly recommended by Samuel Gompers, John Mitchell and others, but was ignored by Mr. Shaffer, head of the Amalgamated Association. About two weeks later a settlement was accepted for a smaller number of mills.[1]

The negotiations before and during the strike of the steel workers show that the company was determined to prevent the spread of unionism, but was not opposed to making contracts for mills already organized.

In defense of this policy, it is generally admitted that when the U. S. Steel Corporation was formed, some of the subsidiary companies which had been non-union, made it a condition of their entering the combine, that the open shop policy would be continued in their plants. In labor matters it has been the policy of the corporation from its inception, to as far as practicable, allow each subsidiary company to handle its own affairs.

This policy of the U. S. Steel Corporation to treat with

1—Article by Samuel Gompers, American Federationist, October 1901. Copies of telegrams and correspondence on file in offices of the National Civic Federation in New York.

existing unions where they were in control and to discourage
the extension of their influence was shown a second time in
the conferences described in the preceding chapter. Mr. Corey
was willing that the American Bridge Company should continue to employ union structural ironworkers on contract
work, as it had been doing before the strike. He was unwilling
to concede the union the erection of the McKeesport tube
mill, which would have been an extension of its sphere of influence.

The unionizing of the McKeesport tube mill involved about
forty men for a few weeks at most. It does not appear that
the point was of sufficient importance to either side to cause
a permanent disagreement, had there been a sincere desire for
peace.

But the point involved more than appears on the surface.
The practice of the steel companies had been to do work for
their own use with non-union men, except in the case of the
Illinois Steel Company. Had the employment of union ironworkers on the McKeesport tube mill been conceded, it would
have established a precedent that in all probability would
have led to disputes in the future and opened the way for the
structural ironworkers to extend the influence of their organization.

As has been shown, the ironworkers in an arbitration award
gave up their claim to such work in the case of the Pennsylvania Steel Company's ore trestle at Steelton, until it had
become the general custom of steel companies to employ union
men on work of this character. It is true that award was
unpopular with the union ironworkers. It had been approved,
however, by Mr. Buchanan and the new president, Mr. Ryan,
probably felt that he had an opportunity to accomplish something that his predecessor had failed to accomplish and in this
way discredit his personal enemy and strengthen himself with
the rank and file of the union.

In addition to that personal satisfaction, the Philadelphia
convention had given positive instructions to its officers not
to make any settlement until every local grievance was sat-

isfactorily adjusted and the Pittsburgh local was determined to obtain for its members the erection of the tube mill at McKeesport.

It appears that the personal ambition of Mr. Ryan to do better than his predecessor in office was a factor in preventing a settlement. The Executive Board could have assumed responsibility for not adhering strictly to the instructions of the convention. Some six months later, the Executive Board, on the recommendation of President Ryan, allowed union men to work on sub-contracts. The instructions of the convention were as emphatic on that point as on the other, but as a matter of policy and expediency, the Executive Board ignored the instructions and removed the ban on sub-contracts.

There was, of course, some difference between the points involved. In removing the ban on sub-contracts, the Executive Board simply authorized union men to work on any job on which union conditions prevailed, regardless of who had the contract. Waiving claim to the work on the McKeesport tube mill would have meant acquiescence in the company's proposition to do some of its work with non-union men.

If the personal equation was a factor on the union side, it probably was as much so on the side of the company. Mr. Corey is said to have asked his directors to give him full authority to deal with the structural ironworkers as he believed he could bring about a settlement. When he failed he felt chagrined and took the matter as a personal affront. The action of Mr. Ryan and his associates in refusing the compromise offered, is said by some who know Mr. Corey to have caused a change in his attitude toward organized labor so that he refused thereafter to have any dealings with unions.

Whether it was the action of the structural ironworkers that embittered Mr. Corey against labor unions or not, it is a fact that the corporation afterward discontinued contractual relations with the longshoremen and the lake seamen and pursued a policy decidedly antagonistic to labor unions that was not apparent in the earlier years of its history.

There is another point to be considered in connection with

the demand for the erection of the tube mill at McKeesport. The structural ironworkers were on strike against the American Bridge Company. The tube mill was being erected by the National Tube Company. While both were subsidiaries of the U. S. Steel Corporation, it does not follow that the American Bridge Company could dictate to the National Tube Company as to the men it should employ. Mr. Gary says that undoubtedly he had the authority to direct the National Tube Company to employ union ironworkers in the erection of its mill, but such action would have been so entirely unprecedented that he would have been unlikely under any circumstances to issue such an order. It would, he says, have been an interference with the authority of local officers, alike distasteful to them and to him and contrary to the established policy of the larger corporation.

In insisting on the erection of the tube mill, the ironworkers reached out and included something that was not an issue when the strike against the American Bridge Company was called. That such work properly came within the jurisdiction of the union is not disputed, nevertheless the demand was something in the nature of a secondary boycott, or an attempt to unionize the work of one company through another, a policy that has failed more often than it has been successful in labor disputes.

Both Mr. Ziesing and Mr. Ryan agree that in the conference with the officials of the U. S. Steel Corporation, the offer was made to employ union bridgemen on all erection work done by the American Bridge Company on a direct contract or through a sub-contractor. The company would not sign a written agreement embodying all the rules and regulations which ordinarily go with such contracts, but did offer to reduce to writing its proposition to employ union men exclusively, pay the recognized wages and work the uniform number of hours.

In agreeing to do that the company met substantially the demands which caused the strike and had the union representatives accepted the offer and waived their claim to the erection of the tube mill, they would have won every point for which they struck. In view of these admitted facts, it cannot be said that the company was at that time bent on destroying the structural ironworkers' organization.

The failure to reach an agreement must be set down to the action of the Philadelphia convention in adopting a resolution which gave the officers no discretionary power and the too strict adherence by the officers to that resolution.

Delegates in a convention of a labor union may properly lay down fundamental laws for the guidance of the membership. When they undertake to lay down hard and fast rules, or a line of conduct for the guidance of their officers during a strike, they are apt to make a serious blunder. Successful prosecution of a war, or a strike, demands centralized authority.

The experience of the ironworkers in dealing with large corporations, may have taught them to hesitate before placing absolute power in the hands of their officers, but there seems little doubt that the failure to do so, prevented a settlement of the strike in October, 1905, and brought on the open shop warfare in the structural iron industry, which five years later attracted the attention of the entire country.

Mr. Ryan has been criticised for not accepting the settlement offered. He might have done so in spite of the orders of the convention and succeeded afterward in justifying his action in the eyes of his constituents. It is not at all certain, however, that he could have so justified his conduct, for the ironworkers at that time were intoxicated with power and Mr. Ryan and his Executive Board believed they could win everything for which they were contending.

If they could have foreseen the results, they would no doubt have acted differently. It is much easier, however, to look backward and criticise than to look forward and anticipate. Mr. Ryan tried to have the Pittsburgh local change its position on the McKeesport job, but when the local refused he stopped there. A better general might have settled in spite of the protest of a single local, when larger interests were at stake. There were ways through which a single local could easily have been brought to time by the international. But Mr. Ryan was too conscientious to go against the expressed instructions of the convention and so committed a fatal blunder.

Samuel Gompers, president of the American Federation of Labor, considers this mistake one of the three most costly blunders made in recent years in the American labor movement. The others were made by Theodore Shaffer when he rejected the offer made before the steel strike in 1901 and by Sam Small when in 1907 he rejected a settlement that could have been obtained for the commercial telegraphers from the telegraph companies.[1]

1—Interview with Mr. Gompers.

CHAPTER VIII.

INDIRECT CAUSES OF OPEN SHOP WAR.

In the preceding chapter it has been shown that the direct cause of the break in contractual relations between the American Bridge Company and the structural ironworkers' organization, was the demand that the erection of a tube mill at McKeesport be done with union men.

Had this point been conceded, it would have meant the extension of the jurisdiction of the union to work that it hitherto had not been able to control, except in the plants of the Illinois Steel Company at South Chicago and Joliet.

It was this extension of power and influence that the company most feared. The erection of the tube mill in itself was of little importance, involving the employment of some forty men for a short time. But the concession if granted, might have proved an entering wedge for still further trespass on what the company regarded as sacred domain. Give the union an inch and it will try to take a yard, was the way the company officials looked at the matter. They feared the unionizing of their fabricating shops and possibly through them of their rolling mills.

The American Bridge Company fabricates on an average about 35 per cent of all the structural steel manufactured in the country. In 1913 it fabricated 47 per cent of the structural steel contracted for that year. The amount of its operations varies according to trade conditions, but since 1905 it has erected on an average less than one-fourth the tonnage it has fabricated and shipped. The following table of figures furnished by President Ziesing of the company, shows the extent of its operations:

STATEMENT OF TONNAGE SHIPPED AND ERECTED BY THE AMERICAN BRIDGE COMPANY SINCE 1905.

Year	Shipped	Erected
1905	407,238	100,732
1906	554,326	115,149
1907	591,653	184,164
1908	342,141	114,548
1909	457,138	43,664
1910	499,794	138,735
1911	501,032	74,629
1912	561,821	101,346
1913	620,500	174,932
1914, to Sept. 30	403,633	

From a business point of view the American Bridge Company would not care if it did not erect any structural steel. Erection work, as explained by Mr. Ziesing, is merely incidental, and is carried on as a business precaution to protect the company's larger manufacturing interests. The company maintains an erecting force and equipment to guard against the possibility of erectors combining and refusing to handle its manufactured products. Without an erecting force the company might be placed at the mercy of erectors, or at least in a less advantageous business position than it now occupies. With its own erecting force the company is in a position to bid on a bridge, or the structural steel in a building erected complete, thus insuring the use of its manufactured products. Its policy is to sub-let erection work, especially on buildings, although even then, it is the largest erector of structural steel in the country.

The International Association of Bridge and Structural Ironworkers claims jurisdiction over the men employed in the fabrication of structural steel in the shops. It has made several unsuccessful efforts to organize different shops of the American Bridge Company. There are a few small locals of shop men affiliated with the International Association at the present time. The reason that all the shop men are not organized, is that it has been found impossible of accomplishment.

Some of the building trades unions, notably the sheet metal workers, carpenters and marble workers, control the men in the shops in their respective crafts. Why not the structural ironworkers? That was the thought uppermost in the minds of the officials of the American Bridge Company when discussing terms of settlement of the strike.

If the structural ironworkers had complete control of erection work, it would be a natural step for them to take advantage of that situation to force the unionizing of the shops. Refusal to handle steel fabricated by non-union men would be a natural and powerful lever to use. Were the shops organized refusal on the part of the men to handle steel rolled in non-union mills would not be entirely illogical. It would be highly improbable, because the workmen in the steel mills do not come under the jurisdiction of the structural ironworkers, but the officials of the steel companies do not overlook probabilities or possibilities.

It is true the structural ironworkers have never refused to erect non-union made material to aid the shop men, but the reason is that they have not considered it practicable to do so. They do not deny the desirability of such action if the chances of success looked favorable. Most of the agreements which they have with employers guard against such sympathetic action by providing that there shall be no restriction of the use of manufactured material. Such a clause in an agreement is in itself an admission of the possibility, and were the ironworkers in a position to do so, they probably would not sign agreements containing such clauses.

In view of the possibilities in the situation and in the light of the well established policy of the U. S. Steel Corporation and its subsidiaries to limit the scope of union activity, it can readily be understood why the company hesitated about conceding to the union the erection of the McKeesport tube mill, or any other point that would widen the union sphere of influence.

Mr. Ziesing is very certain that the union representatives made threats that they would organize the shops and refuse to handle steel rolled in non-union mills. He is certain also, that the union representatives asked that the company should not sell steel to firms employing non-union men in erection work.

Mr. Ryan is equally certain that no such threats or demands were made. He says it would have been ridiculous to have made such demands, as the ironworkers had always handled non-union made material coming from smaller concerns, and if they meant to change that policy they would be unlikely to start with the largest corporation in the industry, which offered the least chance of success.

Assuming that Mr. Ziesing and Mr. Ryan have both told the truth to the best of their recollection, as to what transpired in the conferences, there is only one plausible explanation of the conflicting statements. The conferences took place nine years ago and it would be difficult, if not impossible for any one of the participants to remember clearly all the points discussed, especially as the conferences lasted two days. It is reasonable, therefore to assume that each one would remember most distinctly the particular points which most impressed him at the time.

In a long discussion in which seven men participated, it is entirely probable that many points were brought up which created a different impression on the minds of those who heard them. If the union representatives spoke of refusing to handle non-union made material, or asked the company not to sell steel to non-union erectors, they knew they were asking for something they did not expect to get. That being the case they would regard such points as trivial and incidental and might forget a week afterward that they had been discussed. They would attach no importance to them, but might advance them to offset some points advanced on the other side. The things they did expect to get, such as a written agreement and the erection of the McKeesport tube mill, they would not be apt to forget, as in their minds those things were fundamental.

This explanation appears the more plausible from the fact that today Mr. Ziesing has hardly any recollection of the dispute over the erection of the tube mill and thinks it was one of the little incidental demands. Mr. Ryan on the other hand, says it was the only matter of importance on which no understanding could be reached and was the real cause of the break in relations and his memory on that would be apt to be much better than Mr. Ziesing's.

It is Mr. Ryan's opinion that the points raised by Mr. Ziesing, were in reality advanced by Mr. Mitchell, the chief engineer of the company, to prevent a settlement. He blames Mr. Mitchell for the break between the company and the union. This is disputed by Mr. Ziesing, who was Mr. Mitchell's superior officer. Had Mr. Ziesing been fully satisfied, Mr. Mitchell could not have prevented a settlement.

But Mr. Ziesing was not satisfied and he frankly states that the reason was very largely the fear of union interference in the fabricating shops and with the sale of manufactured materials. He says the ironworkers have several times tried to organize the shops of the company, so that the threat did not appear as idle to him as it might have appeared to the union representatives.

The possibilities in the situation were great enough in the eyes of the company officials to cause them to positively refuse to give the union men the erection of the McKeesport tube mill, which might have proved an entering wedge.

As a matter of choice the company always preferred to work open shop. In well organized centers it made agreements with the unions as a matter of expediency. Even when the company was working under agreements with the local unions. Mr. Ziesing says there were times when it was necessary to hire non-union men, because the union could not always furnish men to meet the company's requirements.

The operations of the American Bridge Company differ materially from those of a large contracting firm, whose activities are restricted to large cities where labor always is available. In taking a contract for a bridge in some isolated part of the country, the company frequently was obliged to find non-union men, as the union could not always find men willing to go. After having organized a gang of bridgemen or "floaters" who were ready to go anywhere, the company was unwilling to discharge such gangs. Its policy was to keep them as much as possible in territory where no local union had jurisdiction, but there were times when that could not be done and trouble arose with a union where a nonunion gang came within the jurisdiction of a local. That appears to have been one of the causes of friction when the company worked under an agreement with the union.

Another cause of friction was the practice of the company to employ laborers in the erection of false work. On isolated jobs where open shop conditions prevailed, there was, of course, no objection raised to this practice. When the company sought to erect false work with laborers within the jurisdiction of a local union, there would immediately be a protest and sometimes a strike. The union ironworkers have always contended for the control of false work and it has been conceded them wherever union conditions prevail.

Such restrictions naturally made the company prefer open shop conditions as a matter of choice, so that at the time of the final break there were a number of influences which strengthened the company's determination to sever its relations with the union. The erection of the McKeesport tube mill furnished the direct pretext and put the company in a defensive position, because hitherto the union had not been able to control such work.

CHAPTER IX.

Post & McCord Strike in New York.

Up to the time that negotiations were broken off between the union and the American Bridge Company, the strike had not effected New York with respect to sub-contracts.

The firm of Post & McCord in that city, was commonly supposed to be a part of the American Bridge Company, although it was denied by members of the firm. Some years before the firm of Post & McCord had sold its fabricating shops to the American Bridge Company and confined its operations to erection work. It purchased all its structural steel from the American Bridge Company.

That there was a close connection between the two companies was admitted, but that the firm of Post & McCord was a part of the American Bridge Company was not established. That the New York local union of ironworkers was working under an agreement with the firm of Post & McCord, as a member of the local association of steel erectors, is not disputed by any one.

Mr. Ryan went to New York and asked the local union to declare a strike on Post & McCord's jobs, on the ground that it was a subsidiary of the American Bridge Company. While some of the local officers did not think the action wise, there was no objection offered in the meeting of the district council when the strike order was passed. Even then the local business agent Charles Massey hesitated to call the strike and told Mr. Ryan that he believed it would be a losing fight.

Mr. Ryan said the Cleveland local had been suspended for not obeying the strike order and that he would not play any favorites. Unless the strike was called, he said, he would suspend the local. The strike on the Post & McCord work was called on November 1, 1905.

The structural ironworkers' union was at that time represented on the General Arbitration Board of the Building Trades Employers' Association and the building trades' unions. The firm of Post & McCord protested against the calling of the strike, in violation of its agreement with the union and a meeting of the representatives of the employers and unions in other trades was called November 3d. The ironworkers were ordered to return to work and they refused.

Some further efforts were made to induce the ironworkers to return to work, the point being raised by the employers that there was no evidence that the firm involved was connected with the American Bridge Company and that the local agreement prohibited the calling of such strikes.

Mr. Ryan insisted that he had proof that the firm of Post & McCord was in reality the American Bridge Company operating under another name in New York City and that any agreement made by a local was not binding when the international ordered a strike.

A meeting of the General Arbitration Board was held on November 16th and a resolution was adopted directing the ironworkers to return to work and that the question of whether the firm of Post & McCord was a part of the American Bridge Company be submitted to a special board, such board to give a decision not later than November 18th. This resolution was adopted by a unanimous vote of 46 on the employers' side and 32 for and 10 against on the union side.

The ironworkers refused to return to work, and the special board to determine the status of the firm of Post & McCord was not appointed. The ironworkers were then suspended from the General Arbitration Board.[1]

The suspension of the ironworkers, with the practically unanimous consent of the other building trades unions, may have been influenced by the fact that it was the second time within a few months that they had gone out on strike in violation of their agreement with their employers. In July, 1905, the ironworkers struck on the Commercial Cable Building in New York against Milliken Brothers, because members of a riggers' union were employed by another firm on the same job to erect smokestacks. On that occasion they were ordered to

---

1—Records of the Building Trades Employers' Association.

return to work, but it took them several days to comply with the order.[1] When they struck the second time, the employers were ready to take drastic action and most of the unions were willing to acquiesce.

At the time the ironworkers were suspended from the General Arbitration Board, they were preparing to demand a wage increase on the expiration of their agreement January 1, 1906. The wages paid at the time were $4.50 a day and the men were asking for $5 a day. This increase being refused, the men struck involving practically all the erectors in New York, including the members of the National Erectors' Association.

This strike appears to have galvanized into action the National Erectors' Association, which up to that time had pursued a non-aggressive policy. While it had members in some other cities, New York was its chief stronghold and as the New York local of ironworkers had placed itself outside the support of other unions in the building trades, the time seemed advantageous to inaugurate an open shop policy.

The National Erectors' Association looked for a man to direct the open shop campaign and finally selected Mr. Walter Drew. He was a young attorney who had previously been the secretary of a Citizens' Alliance in Grand Rapids, Mich. and had given some study to the methods of labor unions and had written a good deal on the subject. He was thoroughly imbued with the open shop idea, and the injustices of the closed shop so-called, as he viewed it. He drafted a constitution for the government of the Association in which the open shop principle was emphasized and convinced the members of the executive committee that it was feasible and practicable to establish and maintain the open shop in the structural iron trade.

The American Bridge Company had, of course, been operat-

1—Records of Building Trades Employers' Association. The ironworkers made application to be re-admitted to the General Arbitration Board May 21, 1906, but the employers objected and no action was taken on the application. The union has never been able to get another agreement with the New York employers.

ing on the open shop basis since the strike against it was called some months previously and as it was the dominating force in the Erectors' Association, Mr. Drew did not find it so difficult to bring the other members to his point of view. The New York employers were bitter against the union, while the ironworkers did not appear to have many friends among the other unions. The declaration for the open shop was made formally on May 1, 1906.

Conditions in the structural iron trade were in a rather chaotic state in the spring of 1906. Employers friendly to the union believed that the wage increase demanded was in excess of what trade conditions warranted and they were unwilling to pay it. A series of conferences were held between those friendly firms most of whom were general contractors, and the union representatives and finally a settlement of the local strike was reached on the basis of 60 cents an hour, or $4.80 a day. Some six or eight firms agreed to the compromise and the ironworkers returned to work for them. The others, however, stood firm against granting any increase, or making any agreement with the union. In fact they refused to meet the union representatives to discuss a settlement and after a time the firms who had agreed to pay $4.80 a day, returned to the former scale of $4.50 and open shop conditions prevailed generally in New York City.

For the next year or two the open shop campaign was actively pushed by Mr. Drew. A great deal of printed matter was issued from the offices of the Association. It was a practice to put circulars in the pay envelopes of the open shop employees, advising them that they did not need a union card and if asked for one on any job, to notify Mr. Drew and their statements would be regarded as confidential. They were informed through these circulars that there was not the slightest possibility of any of the open shop firms recognizing the union, the dynamiting outrages occurring about that time having the effect of making the employers more determined in that respect.[1]

1—Circular issued by Mr. Drew September 15, 1908.

The New York local also was active and frequently issued circulars in answer to those issued by Mr. Drew. In 1908 the union filed a complaint under the Prevailing Wage Law of New York against the McClintic-Marshall Company for paying less than the prevailing wages on the erection of some of the Chelsea piers. The union complaint was based on the fact that the company was employing cheap labor in assembling and shifting material around on the ground, that on a union job would have been done by skilled bridgemen. When actual erection work was started, the company paid the union rate of pay. After an investigation by the comptroller's department, the complaint was dismissed, as it was not found that the law had been violated.

When the union filed the complaint, William Green, who was president and business agent of the New York local asserted that Mr. McClintic, president of the company had offered to employ union men to the extent of 75 per cent of the total working force and to "take care of Green financially" if he would withdraw the complaint. Mr. Green refused the offer and alleged bribe.[1]

In another circular dated October 22d Mr. Drew denied that any bribe had been offered Green, stating that as the comptroller's department had decided there was no violation of the law, there could have been no purpose in seeking to bribe anyone. Of course the decision was not given until several weeks had elapsed after the complaint was filed, so that a bribe might have been offered to have the complaint withdrawn. At least so Mr. Green asserted in a second circular issued November 17th in which he challenged Mr. McClintic to make an affidavit that the charge was untrue.

While the fight was going on in New York the ironworkers received no increase in wages, although wages had been advanced in Boston, Chicago, Cleveland, St. Louis and other large cities.

In December, 1909, the Iron League Erectors' Association

1—Circular issued by New York Union October 5, 1908.

of New York and the National Erectors' Association sent out the following announcement with respect to wages:

"On February 1, 1910, the rate of wages for competent, all around bridgemen and structural ironworkers in New York City paid by members of this Association will be raised to 60 cents an hour and on July 1, 1910, to $5 a day.

"Although no demand upon us had been made from any source, we believe that trade conditions and future prospects justify such increases. The open shop, which we are more than ever determined to maintain, has brought about healthier and better conditions in our industry and in the relations between employers and employees and it is these which have enabled us to take this action at this time.

"We ask the continued confidence and cooperation of our men in the future as in the past. These things mean greater results from the joint efforts of the employer and his men and make possible better returns for both."[1]

This increase in wages is the only one which the structural ironworkers in New York have received in more than twelve years.

---

[1]—Records on file offices National Erectors' Association.

CHAPTER X.

The policy of the structural ironworkers with respect to sub-contracts differs from that usually pursued by other unions in the building industry. Most of the unions are interested only in securing the work for their members, and if a contract has been awarded to a non-union firm and is later sub-let to a union firm, the union is satisfied. There is a certain piece of work to be done, and if it is done under union conditions, the average union in the building trades does not concern itself about who held the original contract.

The reason that the ironworkers pursued a different policy, probably, is due to the fact that they had to deal with large corporations, who might find it convenient to employ union men in one locality and non-union men in another. If the American Bridge Company, for instance, found that it could not employ non-union men on a job, because of the sympathetic action of other unions, it naturally would sub-let the work to some firm that was employing union men. In this way it would be possible to carry on its business with little interruption, employing non-union men where it could do so without interference and sub-letting the work where it could not.

By adopting a policy of working for the American Bridge Company in places where it was compelled by force of circumstances to employ union men, or sub-let its work, the ironworkers could not hope to completely organize the erection work of the company. They, therefore, made a stand for all the work, or none. In doing so they antagonized union firms for whom they had always worked. They over-estimated their own strength and risked losing, probably three-fourths of the work of the company, for the sake of controlling the other fourth.

That this had been the policy of the structural ironworkers, before the last strike against the American Bridge Company was called, or before Mr. Ryan became international presi-

dent, is shown by the records of the organization. The cause
of the strike, as stated, was the awarding of a sub-contract to
a non-union firm.

As previously stated Secretary McNamara in "Circular No.
30 To Local Unions" clearly outlined the policy of the organization in the following language: "No local union should
ever allow any work to proceed under the subterfuge that it has
been taken away from the American Bridge Company, as in
the majority of cases this is but a move to out-wit our local
unions."

The wisdom of risking so much already secured, in the hope
of obtaining a little that for a time seemed beyond reach,
may well be questioned. Experienced labor leaders would
have hesitated, preferring to hold on to what they had and
reach out for more from time to time as a favorable opportunity presented itself. Had the ironworkers adopted that policy,
the open shop campaign of the employers would in all probability have failed before it was fairly started. In the language
of one of the officials of a local union of ironworkers, the policy
resulted in the union "being shot to pieces" in the first few
months of the fight.

In New York, Philadelphia, Chicago, Cleveland and other
large cities, structural iron work that was proceeding under
union conditions, was stopped in pursuance of this policy.
In some instances at least, there was nothing more than a
suspicion that such work was originally contracted for by the
American Bridge Company. From the most reliable information obtainable, the firm of Post & McCord in New York, is
not, nor ever was, a part of the American Bridge Company.
The strike on the work of that firm started the open shop war
in New York and forced other concerns into it that otherwise
might have kept aloof.

In Chicago the union ironworkers were called out of the
plant of the Illinois Steel Company, because like the American
Bridge Company, it was a subsidiary of the U. S. Steel Corporation. It carried on its own erection work independently,
however, and as has been shown, it was the only steel plant of

consequence in the country that employed union structural ironworkers inside its grounds. The stopping of these men could have had little or no bearing on the strike against the American Bridge Company. The men were receiving union wages and working under union conditions and they were informed that if they quit they would not be re-employed.

Some of the leaders in the Chicago union saw the danger in going too far afield in the prosecution of the strike and they opposed calling the men off the Illinois Steel Company's work. Among those was Frank Buchanan, the former international president. Mr. Buchanan said it would result in the union losing work that it then controlled without having any effect on the strike. Mr. Ryan made an appeal to the membership to "beware of the white shirt fellows" meaning Mr. Buchanan, who was not working at his trade at the time. The appeal won and the men were called out. They have been out ever since.

The firm of Kelly-Atkinson Company in Chicago also suffered as a result of the policy of the ironworkers on sub-contracts. The firm had a contract for the erection of part of an elevated railroad. There appeared some doubt as to whether the American Bridge Company was the original contractor. Mr. Buchanan on August 22, 1905, while he was still international president, wrote a letter to Secretary McNamara stating that he had investigated reports that the Kelly-Atkinson work was a sub-contract from the American Bridge Company and he was of the opinion that the reports were not correct.[1]

Mr. Ryan made a second investigation after he assumed office and found that the work was a sub-contract. At least he ordered a strike on the work and kept it tied up for several months, until the Executive Board lifted the ban on sub-contracts.

In Philadelphia the Ettor Erecting Company was building an elevated railroad and employing union men. It was a sub-contract from the American Bridge Company. The union men

---

1—Exhibit No. 7, p. 1104, Vol. 2 Transcript of Record, U. S. Circuit Court of Appeals in Dynamite Conspiracy Cases.

were called off, in spite of the protests of the local union officers. The American Bridge Company finished the work with open shop men.

So far as can be seen this policy of calling strikes on sub-contracts did not hamper the American Bridge Company in the slightest degree. It did have the effect of antagonizing firms that had employed union men and wished to continue doing so. It is difficult to conceive of a policy better calculated to strengthen the position of the open shop employers. The union played into their hands. Some members of the union, forbidden to work on sub-contracts, left the organization and went to work on open shop jobs, exactly as many of the steel workers did in the strike of 1901. The American Bridge Company controlled too much work, either directly or through sub-contractors for the union to place a ban on it all. There was not enough work left to keep the members of the union employed, so it was inevitable that in time some of them would seek employment in spite of the union.

Had the union permitted its members to work on any job where union conditions prevailed, whether a sub-contract from the American Bridge Company or not, it would not have been possible for the open shop firms to obtain the number of experienced ironworkers that they did obtain in the first six months of the fight. If work was to go on and if union men refused to do it, other men had to be found. In a trade where the wages paid are as high, and the degree of skill required as low as that of the structural ironworker, it always is possible to get workmen.

That this policy of refusing to allow union men to work on sub-contracts taken from the American Bridge Company, was a mistake, was admitted by officials of the union themselves after an experience of a few months. In May, 1906, some nine months after the strike was called, the Executive Board, acting on the advice of President Ryan, authorized local unions to allow their members to work on sub-contracts, provided the work was done under union conditions.

While this change in policy improved conditions for the

union ironworkers in some cities, it came too late to repair the damage already done. New York City by that time was practically lost to the union and its influence had been greatly weakened in other places. The business agent of the Philadelphia local said that during the time the ban was in force on sub-contracts, the union in that vicinity lost 60 per cent of its influence.

Shortly after permission was given local unions to allow their members to work on sub-contracts, a movement was started among them to obtain what they termed "local option," which meant permission to work for any open shop firm in a given locality, if given union conditions, regardless of the fact that such firm might be employing non-union men in some other locality.

Delegates from New York, Brooklyn and Philadelphia went to the headquarters of the international union in Indianapolis in February, 1907, to urge the Executive Board to authorize the "local option" policy. Their argument was that they could force some open shop firms to employ union men in their respective jurisdictions. There is no doubt that in the first few months of the fight, some open shop firms would have agreed to employ union men exclusively in certain districts. Architects and owners of buildings who wished to avoid labor difficulties, would not let contracts to open shop firms, where there was danger of other unions joining in sympathetic strikes. This limited the opportunities of the open shop firms in some cities, so that as a matter of business they would have agreed to union conditions on some jobs.

The Executive Board would not consider such a policy. Mr. Ryan was very emphatic against it. He contended that if a local was permitted to follow such a policy in its own jurisdiction, without regard to other locals less favorably situated, there would be no use in having an international union. He could not see the force of the arguments of the "local option" advocates, that if one local controlled conditions within a radius of twenty-five or fifty miles and other locals controlled for like distances, the open shop employers would be hemmed into restricted areas.

From a union standpoint no doubt Mr. Ryan was right, but the open shop employers were steadily gaining ground and it might have been good tactics to restrict their activities wherever it was possible. It is true that through fear of sympathetic strikes and sometimes political influences, the open shop employers occasionally lost a contract that they would have obtained had they employed union men, but the gains they made through steadily increasing the number and efficiency of their open shop working forces, more than offset the occasional losses of contracts which they sustained.

The "local option" question was a subject of controversy and discussion at each convention of the ironworkers for several years. Because of the peculiar conditions in New York, which was entirely open shop, inasmuch as no signed agreements existed, the local there in 1908 received permission to allow its numbers to work on open shop jobs. All the iron erectors in the city except a few general contractors, were working on the open shop plan, so that it appeared to be a necessity to permit the union ironworkers to work by the side of open shop men to preserve what was left of the organization.

Although the "local option" advocates kept up their fight in each convention, it was not until the convention in Indianapolis in February, 1913, that the policy was adopted. It did not work as successfully as its advocates had hoped. According to the opinions of some local officers in open shop territory, the policy resulted in weakening instead of strengthening the union.

The theory of the "local option" advocates proved wrong in 1913 but it does not follow that it might not have been right in 1907 when it was first proposed. At that time there were fewer open shop men in the trade and many of those had limited experience. Each year that passed gave the open shop employers an advantage, by enabling them to train their non-union forces to greater efficiency. By 1913 the open shop policy had been firmly established in the bridge building branch of the trade and in the construction branch in a number of cities. It was too late for the union to overcome the advantage the employers had gained.

The plan followed in New York City of allowing union men to work by the side of open shop men did not bring the results that the union hoped for. It was expected that by permitting union men to work on the same jobs with open shop men, the latter could be induced to join the union. Instead of the open shop men joining the union, many of the union men left the organization and took chances with the open shop forces. The open shop men always were in a majority on a job, so that the influence of the union men was practically nil. The employers did not permit stewards on the jobs and if any coercion was attempted by active union men, they were promptly reported to the employer and discharged.

In the convention held in Peoria, Ill., in September, 1914, resolutions were introduced declaring the "local option" policy a failure and providing for a return to the old conditions. After a long discussion the resolutions were amended to give discretionary power to the Executive Board.

As finally adopted the resolution read:

"Resolved, that this convention in executive session instructs the General Executive Board to order to cease work for any firm that is unfair to any other local union, when after investigation they deem it for the best interests of the International Association."[1]

1—Convention Proceedings, Bridgemen's Magazine, October, 1914.

CHAPTER XI.

Policies of Employers in Open Shop War.

In their fight to establish and maintain the open shop principle in the erection of structural steel and iron, the employers pursued wiser tactics during the crucial period than did their union opponents. They adopted no hard and fast rules of policy, but adapted themselves to circumstances and acted as seemed most expedient.

After the National Erectors' Association announced its open shop policy on May 1, 1906, its members did not deviate from that policy to the extent of holding any formal conferences with union representatives, or entering into any agreements with them. But they had no objections to employing union men if they could find any willing to work for them. Neither did they hesitate to sub-let contracts to firms employing union men, if that plan appeared to offer any advantage.

As the open shop fight progressed and the non-union workmen increased in number and efficiency, the leading firms in the Erectors' Association became a little more strict in the matter of letting sub-contracts to firms employing union men under closed shop agreements. Preference was given to open shop firms and in some instances cash bonds were required to guarantee that the work would be done on the open shop principle.

In numerous instances, however, sub-contracts containing an open shop clause were awarded, with full knowledge that matter of letting sub-contracts to firms employing union men rules. If a union firm was the lowest bidder on a sub-contract, the members of the Erectors' Association were inclined to look at the business side of the proposition and wink at a violation of the open shop principle. An open shop clause in the contract probably eased their consciences, but they did not let their principles stand in the way of profits.

There were occasions when even the open shop clause was

omitted in the awarding of sub-contracts, when the successful bidder was a responsible firm employing union men. The Snare & Triest Company was given sub-contracts in New York by the American Bridge Company and the Pennsylvania Steel Company and the open shop question was not raised. The firm employed union men exclusively on such contracts.[1]

This firm erected two of the Chelsea piers on a sub-contract from the Pennsylvania Steel Company when the open shop fight was at its height in New York and employed only union men. The McClintic-Marshall Construction Company erected the other piers at the same time with open shop men.

The American Bridge Company sub-let the erection of the approaches to a bridge over the East River in New York to the Oscar Daniels Company, knowing that the firm employed union men. The work was completed under union rules.

It appears, however, that the American Bridge Company was stricter in the matter of sub-contracts than some of the other large firms in the Erectors' Association. The New York firm of Terry & Tench was the successful bidder on a sub-contract for the erection of the Madison Avenue Bridge in New York City in 1907. The American Bridge Company insisted on an open shop clause in the contract. Terry & Tench had no objections, it being the intention of the firm to accept the clause and employ union men exclusively as it had been doing up to that time.

Mr. Drew, the commissioner of the Erectors' Association, was asked for an opinion if such an open shop clause was enforceable. He said it was not, but that he would draw up a clause that would meet the requirements. He accordingly drew up a clause providing that an agent of the Erectors' Association be allowed to visit the work and hire or discharge men to insure the job being done under open shop rules. Terry & Tench would not accept such a clause and the contract was canceled.[2]

The Pennsylvania Steel Company let a sub-contract for the

1—Statement of Arthur W. Buttenheim, Secretary of the Company.
2—Statements of Mr. Tench and Mr. Drew.

erection of a viaduct to J. H. Greiner, a Philadelphia contractor who was employing union men. He was required to put up a cash bond of $6,000 that the work would be done on the open shop plan. He did not wish to get into trouble with the union, while at the same time he wanted to get the contract. The matter was quitely arranged with the business agent of the Philadelphia union and Mr. Greiner started work with an open shop force. Gradually the open shop men were found to be "incompetent" and discharged. The union business agent saw to it that union men were on hand to fill the places. In three weeks the job was entirely unionized and it was finished before the Pennsylvania Steel Company knew of the arrangement. Mr. Greiner, however, did not get another sub-contract from that company or any other member of the Erectors' Association and soon afterwards joined the union and went to work at the trade.[1]

The Strobel Steel Construction Company of Chicago took a good many sub-contracts from the American Bridge Company and at one time was a member of the Erectors' Association. It employed union men exclusively and when it persisted in this policy it was expelled from the Erectors' Association.[2]

The National Erectors' Association never imposes any penalties in the shape of fines on its members for violations of the open shop principle to which they are pledged. They are expected to live up to the open shop rule on all work done by them directly, and as far as possible see that any work sub-let by them is carried on in the same way. Occasional lapses from the rule are overlooked, but if a firm persists in ignoring the rule so that it is apparent that it is not trying to observe it, that firm is dropped from membership.

It has been charged by union officials that the National Erectors' Association has coerced some firms into declaring for the open shop. It has been shown that the members of the

---

1—Statement of M. J. Cunnane, Business Agent Philadelphia Local.
2—Statement of Mr. Drew.

Erectors' Association control the output of approximately 75 per cent of the fabricated steel used. The American Bridge Company alone fabricated 35 per cent or more, so that it would appear plausible that pressure might be brought to bear on some erectors through this control of manufactured material.

There does not appear to be any foundation for these charges, at least through the control of manufactured material. Any reputable contractor finds no difficulty in obtaining material. The competition among the steel companies is too keen to permit of any discrimination on account of the employment of union or non-union men in erection work. Complaints of this nature when carefully followed up were, without exception, found to be without merit.

A seemingly well authenticated case was learned in New York City, where a large general contracting firm which employs union men, was said to have had trouble with the American Bridge Company in the way of procuring material. Investigation proved that the trouble arose over an entirely different matter and that it was the general contractor, who for business and personal reasons, quit purchasing material from the company. It was not a case of the company refusing to sell or make prompt delivery, but of the contractor refusing to buy.

This particular firm is not on friendly business relations with the American Bridge Company and when its manager said that he had never heard of the company refusing to sell, or delay the delivery of material on account of the employment or non-employment of union ironworkers, it may be assumed he was not speaking in defense of the company. As a matter of fact he scouted the idea as ridiculous and said that any one familiar with conditions in the structural iron trade would know that such a charge could not be true.[1]

Officials of the American Bridge Company have stated that in their last conference with the representatives of the structural ironworkers' union, the latter asked the company not to sell material to firms employing non-union men in erection

1—Statement of Mr. Rowan, Manager James Stewart Co. New York.

work. Mr. Gary said that such action would render the company liable to prosecution for conspiracy. The same would hold true if the company refused to sell to firms employing union men and if it tried to delay deliveries it would lose the business. The American Bridge Company is in business to sell all the steel it can, and as Mr. Ziesing said, it is not concerned about what is done with the steel after it has been delivered.

Because no coercive tactics have been pursued in the matter of control of manufactured steel, it does not follow that the Erectors' Association has not used pressure on union firms in another direction to have them work open shop. This has been done in the way of refusing to let a sub-contract to a union firm, or by insisting on an open shop clause in such contracts.

If a firm had little work on hand and had a chance to secure a favorable sub-contract from the American Bridge Company, or any other large open shop firm, the business temptation to declare for the open shop and accept the contract would be great. In some instances the temptation was too strong to resist, so that in this way the Erectors' Association did exercise pressure on independent union firms.

On the other hand, if the union could bring sufficient pressure to bear to cause a contract to be taken away from an open shop firm and given to a union concern, it did not hesitate to do so. As a matter of fact the union sometimes succeeded in doing that and hailed it as a victory. If the thing was legitimate in the one case, it was equally so in the other. It was all a part of the fight and in playing the game, the records prove that the employers kept within the law much closer than did their opponents.

While a few firms may have been forced to declare for the open shop to procure contracts, they are exceptions. As a general rule the open shop employers are such from choice. The truth is that many union concerns would prefer to work open shop if they could do so without danger of sympathetic strikes on the part of other unions. Some large general contractors who employ union ironworkers exclusively, contribute to the support of the National Erectors' Association. They do not advertise the fact and are classed as strong advocates of unions, but privately they indorse the open shop campaign. They feel that it has benefited them by keeping the union ironworkers in check. The union is less apt to cause trouble over minor infractions or rules when the possibility is always present of an employer hiring open shop men.

CHAPTER XII.

WHY ERECTORS PREFER OPEN SHOP.

Assuming that the structural iron erectors who have adopted the open shop policy, have done so from choice, it follows that they must have had some business reasons for doing so. What are the reasons?

A great deal of literature has been issued by associations of open shop employers, tending to show that the fight is purely one of principle; that principle being the right of a workman to work where and for whom he pleases and under such conditions as he may see fit.

It is not necessary to waste time or space in discussing that plea. Until society provides a plan for assuring every man, who is able and willing to work, an opportunity of doing so, it is idle to talk about his sacred right to work.

Setting aside, therefore, the thoughtless and many times hypocritical plea of some open shop employers, that they are contending for a fundamental principle, the matter may be discussed from a purely business point of view.

If employers who are fighting for the open shop would frankly admit that they are doing so for business reasons to increase their power and profits, and if labor unions who are fighting the open shop would admit that they are doing so for precisely the same reasons, the public would hear less meaningless twaddle about abstract principles. No matter how many high-sounding phrases may be used in discussing the subject, in the last analysis it is a common, ordinary question of dollars and cents.

In the structural iron trade, New York City furnishes a good illustration of the effect of the open shop on wages. That city is the stronghold of the National Erectors' Association and the wages paid structural ironworkers are lower than in any of the leading cities of the country. They are lower than the wages paid in most of the other building trades in New

York, where the unions are working under contractual relations with their employers.

Not only that, but the wages paid structural ironworkers in New York are 50 cents a day higher than the scale of the Erectors' Association for any other city in the country, which makes the difference between the open shop and the union scale still more marked.

The National Erectors' Association has not issued a wage scale since November, 1912, while the union scale has been raised in a number of cities since that time. The open shop erectors have three different rates of wages applying to all the principal cities in the country. Those rates for an eight-hour workday are $5 in New York City and vicinity, $4.50 a day in seventeen and $4 a day in thirty-four other cities.

It should be said that the rates of the Erectors' Association are standard and as most of the work of its members is bridge work, the differences in some instances may be less than they appear. Some of the unions have a lower road scale than their city scale, so that outside of New York and vicinity, it might be fairer to compare the scale of the Erectors' Association with the road scale of the unions. By doing so the advantage in favor of the Erectors' Association is very slight, as only a few locals have a lower road scale than their city scale.

On the average the wages paid by members of the Erectors' Association are considerably lower than the wages paid by firms employing union men.

The following comparison of the open shop and union scale for structural ironworkers in twelve leading cities in different sections of the country is a fair illustration:

City.	Open Shop Scale. Cents per Hour.	Union Scale. Cents per Hour.
New York	62½	62½
Buffalo	56¼	65*
Chicago	56¼	68
Cleveland	56¼	70
Denver	56¼	56¼
Boston	50	62½*
Minneapolis	50	62½
St. Louis	50	75*
Louisville	50	50
San Francisco	56¼	75*
Indianapolis	56¼	68
Baltimore	56¼	56¼

In comparing open shop with union wages in the structural iron trade, there is one condition that should be considered. The open shop men have more steady employment, which, of course, increases their annual earnings, so that they would more nearly equal the earnings of the union men. The open shop employers strive to keep their gangs steadily employed, while the union employers, doing work in large cities have no difficulty in procuring competent men at any time. The supply of open shop men is more limited, which has a tendency to give them steadier employment.

But aside from the question of the nominal rate of pay per hour, there are other reasons why the erectors prefer the open

*The rate quoted is that claimed by the union, which does not agree with the rate given for those cities by E. M. Craig, secretary of the Building Construction Employers Association of Chicago, whose tables are prepared with great care from information received from various sources. Mr. Craig's figures for 1914 for San Francisco are 62½ cents an hour and for St. Louis 60 cents an hour. The rates shown in Mr. Craig's tables are 62½ cents an hour for Buffalo and 56¼ cents for Boston. The Baltimore scale for 1914 is 50 cents a day lower than the scale for 1913. In St. Louis the scale for structural ironworkers was 65 cents an hour for 1911-12-13 and in 1914 a strike was called for 75 cents an hour. The employers fought the increase and an independent union was formed. The rate claimed by the union may be paid on some jobs. but may not be the standard rate recognized in that locality.

shop. As a matter of fact the open shop employers deny that they pay less than union employers to competent bridgemen. They say they do not object to high wages. What they do object to are the rules and restrictions imposed by the union and the interference of walking delegates. Several large employers who recently turned from union to open shop conditions say they were driven to the change by the actions of some local business agents of the union.

In that respect, however, the question again resolves itself into one of dollars and cents. The union rules and restrictions of which the employers complain, are simply methods used by the union to get more wages for its members, or more work, which is the same thing. The union rules may not mean a higher rate of pay per hour. The minimum rate is generally well established and seldom cause for dispute. It is the jurisdiction of work which causes the real trouble and adds to the cost of construction where the union controls, or reduces the cost where open shop conditions prevail, without changing the standard rate of pay per hour.

One of the chief causes of friction between the American Bridge Company and the union, at the time when contractual relations obtained, was the question of the erection of falsework. The union has always claimed that the erection and removal of falsework is a part of the structural ironworker's trade, and it is so conceded in all agreements that have been made. That means of course, that falsework must be erected and removed by union men, receiving the minimum rate of pay.

On an open shop job the employer may, if he chooses, do such work with unskilled labor. The laborers probably receive about one-half the pay of skilled bridgemen. On a union job the employer would have to pay skilled men to do this class of work, so that it can readily be understood why union ''rules and restrictions'' are objectionable from the employer's point of view. Relieved of such rules, the open shop employer could afford to pay skilled men the highest rate of pay and still profit over his competitor who employed union men.

The erection of falsework, however, requires some degree of skill, so that it does not furnish as clear an illustration of the cost of some union rules, as does the handling of material.

In all agreements made between the union ironworkers and their employers provision is made for laborers handling material in yards and storage points, and for delivering material from such yards and storage points to the site of the work. The site of the work is defined:

(*a*) In the case of buildings, within reach of the derricks, or other appliances used in erecting the materials.

(*b*) In the case of bridges, viaducts and similar structures, to the point of the structure nearest the storage yard.[1]

The agreements provide also that in the removal of old structures laborers may handle the material after it has been dismantled and landed by bridgemen, which means that skilled workmen must do the dismantling and lowering of the material.

The enforcement or non-enforcement of these rules mean a material difference in the cost of erection. The handling of structural iron does not require skill. A sturdy laborer could handle it better than a less sturdy skilled workman.

The erection of a viaduct may be taken as an example of how the rule works. If the work is being done under union conditions, laborers may deliver the material to the point of the structure nearest the storage yard. Suppose the employer decided to establish a storage yard along the side of the viaduct, if the conditions made that practicable, laborers would then be handling the material over the entire length of the viaduct. Suppose again the walking delegate visited the job and stopped the work, demanding that bridgemen handle the material from the point nearest the extreme end of the viaduct. The employer quite naturally would resent such "union interference" as it meant to him the employment of high-priced men to do work that could be satisfactorily performed by laborers. It cuts down his profits, while it in-

---

1—See Agreement Appendix p. 165.

creases the profits of the bridgemen by giving them more work.

Whether the work should be done by the high-priced or the low-priced man, is a matter on which opinions will differ. The employer will, of course, contend that it is uneconomic to pay skilled labor for doing unskilled work, but the union ironworker is not interested in that phase of the subject. His philosophy is that the work should always go to the high-priced man, if he can get it, and he is in a union to help him get it.

One of the largest structural iron firms in New York turned from the union to the open shop in 1913 over the question of handling material. The business agent of the Brooklyn union stopped the work, because laborers were handling material that was claimed to be the work of bridgemen. In speaking of the reasons for declaring for the open shop, a member of the firm complained bitterly of "grafting walking delegates" and said they had driven him to work open shop. It was the rules and regulations of which he complained, not of wages or hours of labor.[1]

Another question which at one time caused friction is the number of men used in a riveting gang. It was the custom to employ four men in a gang, although a literal reading of the union agreements shows that employers could use a fewer number without any violation of the contract. Some of the employers tried to work three men in a gang. Under certain conditions, when the heating furnace was close to the spot where the rivets were to be used, three men might work in a gang with fairly good results. The experiment, however, proved uneconomical and was generally given up after a trial. Practically all firms, whether union or open shop, employ four men in a riveting gang. While the plan was being tested, however, it caused trouble and furnished employers with another instance of "union interference."

Complaints of employers that union stewards on jobs are a

1—Statement of Mr. Tench of the firm of Terry & Tench.

source of trouble and annoyance are probably greatly exaggerated. All the ironworkers' agreements provide that no person not authorized by the employer, shall interfere with workmen during working hours.

Mr. Ziesing says that in his last conference with union representatives a demand was made that the steward be allowed to pass judgment on the reasons for discharging a workman. On that point, Mr. Ziesing probably voiced his fears of something that might be possible, because the ironworkers were unlikely to ask something of the American Bridge Company in that respect, that they did not ask or expect of other employers.

None of the rules and regulations referred to apply on open shop jobs, where the employer is free to do as he likes. The skilled open shop workmen do not like to see laborers doing work which they think bridgemen should do but they are powerless to prevent it. Some of them complain that their trade is being taken away by laborers, which indicates that the desire to control the work is not confined to the union ironworker. The desire is a common one, the difference is that the union ironworker is in a position to gratify that desire and the open shop man is not. A union card does not greatly change human nature. The non-union man of today may be the union man of tomorrow, or *vice versa,* but in matters affecting his own particular trade, he is apt to think pretty much the same way all the time.

In addition to the financial reasons for opposing union rules and regulations, there is the natural human desire to do as one pleases. Some employers resent the idea of being forced to do anything, whether it costs them anything or not. They feel that as they have to pay the fiddler, they should have the right to dictate the tune.

If a city policeman ordered an erector to remove some material from the street because it obstructed traffic, he would comply without question. But if the walking delegate—the policeman of the union—ordered him to remove it with skilled men instead of laborers, he would resent such an interference with his rights.

In the one case the removal would be ordered for the public good; in the other for the good of the union ironworkers, who are a part of the public. In both instances it would be an interference with the right of an individual to do as he pleased.

Because of these rules and restrictions, it is readily seen why the iron erectors prefer the open shop. And by the same token it is easily seen why the union ironworkers oppose it. The employer believes that the union rules interfere with rights that are his by law and custom. The union ironworker knows that the open shop rules restrict his opportunities to earn bread and butter.

CHAPTER XIII.

Why Unions Fight for Closed Shop.

To understand why some unions will stake their very existence to obtain a closed shop agreement, so-called, while other unions are ready and willing to accept open shop contracts, it is necessary to understand something of the peculiar conditions obtaining in the particular trade. It is necessary also to understand the meaning of the term "open shop" for it does not convey the same meaning in every instance.

The building trades unions, without exception, aim at having union or closed shop agreements with their employers. Whatever the actual wording of these agreements may be, they mean that the employer on his part agrees to hire members of the union, and the union on its part obligates itself to supply all the competent workmen needed in the particular line of work. Such agreements are not altogether one-sided, because the employer is assured of having an adequate labor supply at all times to meet his requirements.

These trade agreements mean that a committee representing the employers and a committee representing the workmen, have met in joint conference and drafted certain rules fixing wages and conditions of employment in that particular trade. They mean that both sides recognize the principle of collective, rather than individual bargaining.

Agreements between the railroad companies and the various railroad brotherhoods do not provide for the exclusive employment of union men. The railroad brotherhoods do not assume the responsibility of supplying all the competent men required by the railroads. These agreements are commonly known as "open shop" agreements, and the railroad brotherhoods are quite willing that they should be so regarded. But for all practical purposes they are as effective as the so-called closed shop agreements in the building trades.

Street railway companies frequently make open shop agreements with unions of their employes and the issue of the closed shop is seldom raised. Certainly that issue would not be regarded by the union officials as a sufficient cause for a strike, if it did not involve the question of discrimination against union men. If a street railway company was willing to make a contract with its employees and show no discrimination as between union and non-union men, such a contract would be acceptable to the union.

It is difficult for some to understand why one union will accept an open shop agreement while another will not. Is the building trades workman differently constituted from the locomotive engineer or the street car motorman? Of course, he is not, but he is forced to adopt different tactics to obtain the same results, due to the different conditions in his trade.

Mr. Drew, Commissioner of the National Erectors' Association, says that the structural ironworkers never accepted the open shop principle in good faith, and like hundreds of others, he points to the railroad brotherhoods as conspicuous examples of unions that have accepted the open shop and prospered under the system.

The conditions surrounding the railroad trainman and the building trades workman are entirely different. It has been said that the contracts between the railroad companies and the brotherhoods are for all practical purposes union agreements, as effective as if they were closed shop contracts. The reason is this: The representatives of the railroads meet in conference with the representatives of the brotherhoods and agree on certain schedules of wages and hours for the different classes of men in train service.

Those schedules apply alike to union and non-union men in the different classes. There is no individual bargaining, or no individual cutting of wages once the schedules have been adopted. The adoption of the schedule has at once eliminated the competition of the non-union man. The union men, in other words, have set the standards of employment, which is all that a building trades union does when it makes a closed shop contract.

If the employer in the building trades made an open shop agreement, the union men would not be protected as are the railroad employees from the competition of the non-union man. The contractor might employ union men on one job and non-union men, at a lower rate of pay on another job. Or he might, as he has done in the past, employ union and non-union men on the same job at different rates of pay and in this way break down standards, or prevent them from being established. The opportunities for doing so, in a trade where men are being constantly employed and discharged, are too many, and the building trades workman insists that the competition of the non-union man be eliminated by specific agreement.

It might be possible, of course, for a building contractor to agree to pay certain wages under an open shop agreement, but if he did that the main incentive for desiring an open shop agreement would be removed. He might as well sign a closed shop agreement and that is what he does. Besides trade union agreements are much like civil laws. Their enforcement depends upon the force of opinion behind them. It is well known that a law which is obnoxious to a majority of the people is non-enforceable. An open shop agreement in the building trades would be worthless in practice, no matter how well it may sound in theory. A closed shop agreement is enforceable only because of the organized strength of the workmen behind it.

A closed shop agreement does not mean that the building contractor or his foreman asks a workman on being hired whether he is a member of the union. He hires him and the union steward on the job sees to it that he has a union card, or that he makes application to join. The picture, sometimes painted, of the employer with tears in his eyes telling a workman that he would like to employ him, but cannot do so because he is not a member of the union, is purely fanciful.

The main purpose of the closed shop agreement in the building trades is to give the union power to control conditions, to establish and maintain recognized standards. The union cannot control conditions in the trade, unless it controls the men engaged in that trade.

But there is another reason. The high wages and short workday in the building trades, have been brought about by organized effort. That will not be disputed. The union man therefore does not think that the non-union man, who has not contributed either money or work to improve conditions, should reap a reward that he does not deserve. The good conditions have been brought about in spite of the non-union man. Usually the non-union man has done his best to retard every advance that has been made. In the opinion of the union man his non-union competitor is not entitled to much consideration. The union man does not feel that he is treating his non-union competitor unfairly when he compels him to either join the union and contribute his share to its support, or get off the union job.

It may be said that the same line of reasoning applies to the non-union railroad employee. It does, but the railroad brotherhoods do not have to rely on closed shop agreements to build up and retain their membership. There are other conditions in connection with railroad work that are as impelling as the closed shop agreement in the building trades.

There are three good reasons why the railroad brotherhoods can afford to accept open shop agreements and prosper under them: The first reason has already been alluded to. It is that once the schedule of wages and hours has been adopted it applies to every employee in that line of service and there is no danger of the non-union man breaking down the established standard.

Another reason why the railroad brotherhoods grow in strength and influence without the aid of a closed shop agreement is found in the strict rules of discipline maintained by the railroads. An employe in railroad train service is suspended or discharged for a slight infraction of the rules. If he is a member of a brotherhood, he can appeal to a committee and if he has been unfairly treated, the brotherhood will insist on his reinstatement. If he is not a member he has to fight his own battle and the chances of his reinstatement are slim. The stricter the rules, the more incentive there is for employees joining the brotherhoods for their protection.

The third reason is the insurance features of the railroad brotherhoods. The occupation is a hazardous one and accidents are numerous. The brotherhoods provide insurance for their members at a much lower rate than they could obtain in any other way.

Those factors explain why the railroad brotherhoods do not have to rely on closed shop agreements. The employees bargain collectively under the open shop plan and are given protection by the brotherhoods, both with respect to security in their jobs and insurance against accidents.

There is another factor to be considered and that is the attitude of the employers. Although the railroad brotherhoods are frequently pointed out as examples of successful open shop unions, the railroad company is not a fair example of the open shop employer. All the large railroad systems in the country, with one or two exceptions, recognize the principle of collective bargaining and meet representative committees of their employers to discuss working conditions. This is not the policy of the average open shop employer.

The open shop employer in the structural iron industry, in the metal trades and elsewhere, does not recognize the principle of collective bargaining. Assuming that the open shop is in reality open, that is, that union men can find employment there without discrimination, such union men have no voice in making the conditions of employment. The wages and hours are fixed by the employer, so that the shop is to all intents and purposes non-union. The fact that some members of a union may be employed in that shop does not alter the situation in the slightest degree. If men cannot have a voice in fixing conditions of employment or bargain collectively for the sale of their labor power, they might just as well not be members of a union. Men join unions mainly for practical reasons. If the union cannot help them in a practical way they will not join it.

Open shop advocates who point to the relations between railroad companies and the various railroad brotherhoods to prove their contention, often fail to take the attitude of the railroad companies into consideration. If the railroad brotherhoods are to be contrasted with the unions in the building trades, or in the metal trades, the railroad companies should be contrasted with the employers in those trades.

Recognition of the union is not an issue among the railroad companies. The right of the brotherhoods to legislate for all the employees in their particular line of service, is fully recognized by the companies. The railroad companies, therefore, are not open shop employers in the sense that the members of the National Erectors' Association and the Metal Trades Association are. Those associations do not recognize the right of their employees to bargain collectively. The employees are not permitted to set up the standards for all men engaged in their particular line of work.

On the contrary, these employers refuse to recognize the union in any way. They may employ a union man, in the same way that they might employ a Catholic or a Methodist, but such employment would have no significance. That is the reason why union men commonly refer to the so-called open shop as a "non-union" shop, or as a shop that is "closed" to union men.

CHAPTER XIV.

Building Trades Unions and Restriction of Output.

The relative efficiency of open shop and union workmen has been much discussed and many statements have been made on both sides of the question that are exaggerated and misleading.

It is generally conceded in the building trades, that the best workmen are members of the union in their respective crafts. Even the open shop employers concede that as a general statement. They say, however, that through the power of the union, the workmen restrict output, so that while the union man, as an individual, may be capable of doing more efficient work than the non-union man, he frequently proves, as a matter of fact less efficient.

There is undoubtedly a tendency among members of some unions in the building industry to restrict output under certain conditions. This has been shown in the Eleventh Special Report of the United States Commissioner of Labor (p. 274), the reasons given being the seasonal character of the work and the idea that by going easy the job will last longer.

But if this tendency is admitted, it does not necessarily follow that it is confined to union men. It is much less a question of union rules than it is one of trade conditions at the time. During a season of abnormal activity, when there is a scarcity of men in a particular trade, the output naturally will be somewhat less than in a season of business depression when there are many idle men in the trade. This is equally true on a union or on an open shop job, for the tendency to take things easier when there is a feeling of security in the job, is a human rather than a union one.

In a season of industrial depression, no rules which a union might make are strong enough to prevent the individual workman putting forth his best efforts to hold his job. The competition of the idle man on the street is stronger than any union rule and as the seasons in which there is a scarcity of labor, are exceedingly rare in the building industry, the question of restriction of output is not a serious one. It is, of course, more apparent in some trades than in others, dependent on the supply of labor in the particular trade.

In the structural iron trade, in which about 45 per cent of the work is being done under open shop conditions, the union cannot possibly have a monopoly on the labor supply, so that the opportunity to restrict output is limited, even if the inclination to do so is admitted.

If one listens to the conversation among union ironworkers, as they congregeate around their meeting halls, or in saloons where they gather, he will hear something like this:

"We certainly are making things hum on our job. Stuck up a whole story today. Never saw anything like it."

"Yes, you damned fools and two weeks from now you will be out of a job and wondering how it happened."

Here we have in a snatch of an actual conversation the whole story. There was no restriction of output. On the contrary the job was going too fast to last. The fear of unemployment when the job was finished, which is at the bottom of restriction of output in the building trades, was present, but less ominous than the fear of immediate discharge. If the ironworkers on the job did not "stick up a story a day," the assumption is that the job would not last two days for them. If they did "stick up a story a day," the job would last until it was finished, in a few days or a few weeks as the case might be.

Interviews with members of some large structural iron firms which recently turned from the union to the open shop, showed that there is little foundation for the claim that union men are less efficient than open shop men. On the contrary, those employers said that if there was any difference the advantage lay with the union men. They said the best open shop men they have were former members of the union.

One employer said that when he employed union men exclusively, he had occasionally observed a tendency on the part of a riveting gang to "go a little easy." When he saw such a tendency, he said, that gang was promptly discharged and there would be no more "soldiering" on that particular job. This confirms the statement that the competition for jobs usually is strong enough in the structural iron trade to check any tendency to restrict output.

In some of the literature issued by Mr. Drew, Commissioner of the National Erectors' Association, statements have appeared that a union gang of riveters have driven in a day about one-third the numbers of rivets driven by an open shop gang. Mr. Drew is not an ironworker. He is a lawyer and it is his business to present his case in the most favorable light he can.

But if such statements are accepted at their full face value, they do not prove the greater efficiency of the open shop gang. Any one with practical knowledge of a trade understands how conditions may vary on different jobs, or even on the same job.

To make a comparison between the number of rivets driven in a day on buckle plate on a bridge girder, with the number driven in column splices on a building would be ridiculous. An open shop gang driving rivets in buckle plate on a bridge girder might easily drive 400 rivets a day and not be as efficient as a gang which drove 150 on column splices on a building. There is the difficulty of getting at the work, the raising and lowering of scaffolds and a dozen other conditions, which the practical ironworker, whether a journeyman or an employer, understands.

On the same building the conditions vary so much that it might be quite possible for an open shop gang to make a much better showing than a union gang in the matter of driving rivets. A foreman who was anxious to have an open shop gang make a better showing, could easily arrange it so that they would. If he was a union foreman, the reverse would probably be the case and the union men would show to greater advantage.

To make comparisons that would mean anything, the conditions under which the work was performed would have to be the same. The practical employer or foreman knows what a fair day's work is, and the bridgeman who does not do a fair amount of work, will not last long on any union job.

It is not the practice among the ironworkers, or other unions in the building trades to take up the cause of a discharged workman. The foreman on a job may discharge a man if he does not like the color of his hair and the union will not question such a discharge. All agreements between the ironworkers and their employers, provide that the employer or his representative may discharge any workman as he sees fit.

A general rule among building trades unions, is that the employer may discharge a workman at any time, provided always that he hires another union man to fill the vacancy. Should a workman be discharged for laziness or incompetency and appeal to his union, he would receive little sympathy among his fellows. It is a fact that some building. trades unions have disciplined members for appearing on a job in an intoxicated condition which led to their discharge. Generally speaking, it is not true that a building trades union will compel an employer, through the threat of a strike, to keep on a building any workman whom he may desire to discharge.

If it is true that the employer in the structural iron trade is free to discharge workmen as he sees fit without interference on the part of the union, it follows that there can be no serious restriction of output, unless as stated, there is unusual activity in the trade and competent men are scarce. Such periods of unusual activity are rare and when they occur the open shop man is quite as apt to "ca canny" as is the union man.

There is another factor to be considered in connection with the alleged restriction of output and that is the "pacemaker." The "pacemaker" is less common, perhaps, among the building trades than in the shop or factory, where the opportunities for setting a pace are greater. But he is not unknown in the building trades. He is found in all the unions and is the cause of the adoption of rules prohibiting "rushing."

The "pacemaker" is an exceptionally fast workman, who frequently receives a few cents an hour more than the union scale. Even when he does not receive extra pay for setting a pace for others to follow, he performs more work than the average man, with less physical exertion to himself. He is sometimes described by his fellows as "a natural born mechanic who can make every move count."

In adopting rules against "rushing" as some building trades unions have done,[1] although they are a dead letter in dull seasons, it is not so much the purpose of such rules to restrict the activities of the exceptional man, as it is to protect the average man who cannot maintain the pace, no matter how he may try.

The "rusher" might be allowed to "work his head off" were it not for the fact that one man after another is discharged, because he cannot keep up to the pace. If the foreman would recognize that the "rusher" is an exceptional man and not discharge other men because they are only average, there would be no trouble.

But that is not what the foreman has the "rusher" for. He is there to urge others on by his example, and when the foreman continually refers to the amount of work the "rusher" is doing, the other workmen come to regard him as a common enemy. He is warned to "let up on it" and probably does. The union then is blamed for restricting output. But the foreman is not without blame in the matter also. He brought about the restriction by discharging men who were not able to keep up the pace set by the "rusher."

It is common for an employer to advance a plea that a graded scale of wages would solve the problem, as then men would be paid "what they were worth." It sounds plausible, but it does not work in practice in the building trades. The difficulty about the plan is, who is to determine what a man is worth? The workman is apt to have a very different idea of his worth to that of his employer.

1—Eleventh Special Report, U. S. Commissioner of Labor, p. 272.

Some years ago the union lathers in Chicago adopted a graded scale. Three classes of workmen were created, each with a different wage scale. In a dull season they all became third class workmen and in a busy season they were all first class. The net result was a reduction in wages in dull seasons. The plan was discarded and a uniform minimum scale adopted.

A bonus over the minimum scale has been tried in some trades, but that would not be practicable in the building trades where the work is seasonal. Every man would expect to receive the bonus in busy seasons and no one would receive it in dull seasons. The work of the building mechanic cannot be apportioned with a degree of accuracy that is possible in a shop or factory. In a shop or factory, where the work is minutely sub-divided, hundreds of workers may be performing exactly similar operations, under exactly similar conditions.

In the building trades the facilities for work vary and the operations are seldom exactly the same. It is impossible, therefore, to standardize a day's work as may be done in the shop or factory. The minimum wage scale, adopted by the unions and the employers, appears to be the most practical and equitable method of adjusting wages.

The minimum scale does not reduce all workmen to a "dead level" as is so often asserted. It is true that it protects the average man when he is employed. But in dull seasons it will invariably be found that the less efficient men are out of work. A lower wage scale for the less efficient would not create more work and furnish them employment. It would, however, pull down the wages of the more efficient, who would still continue to do the work, but at a lower rate of pay.

If the unions did not set a minimum scale of wages, the minimum would be set by the necessity of the idle man on the street and standards of living would be lowered. Can society afford to countenance or encourage such a condition? The "dead level" which the minimum scale is sometimes charged with creating is in reality a "living level" which assures the average, or the less efficient workman, a living wage when he is employed. Abolish it and establish a standard set by the necessities of the idle man on the street, and the workers would be reduced to what might in more truth be termed a "dead level."

CHAPTER XV.

Spies in the Ironworkers' Union.

The employment of spies in labor unions is a common practice, especially with large corporations. Espionage is closely related to violence. Sometimes it is the direct cause of violence and where that cannot be charged, it often is an indirect cause.

If the secret agents of employers, working as members of labor unions, do not always instigate acts of violence, they frequently encourage them. If they did not they would not be performing the duties for which they are paid, for they are hired on the theory that labor organizations are criminal in character.

If they find that labor unions are not criminal organizations and that acts of lawlessness never are discussed in union meetings, they have nothing to report to those employing them. If they do not report matters which the detective agencies employing them can carry to corporations to frighten them, it follows that they cannot last long as spies, or "operatives" as they are professionally known.

The very nature of the business, therefore, makes it virtually necessary for the spy to do either of two things. Either he must make reports that are false, in which case discovery would be inevitable sooner or later, or he must create a basis on which to furnish truthful reports. The latter plan is the better suited to his purposes, and he governs himself accordingly.

Whether the particular act of lawlessness he has in mind is an attack on non-union workmen, or the destruction of property, he will not find it impossible in any union, at least in the building trades, to find some who are ready to listen to him.

Men who engage in this kind of work are not troubled with conscientious scruples. They should not be confused with real detectives, whose business it is to prevent the commission of crime, or bring the perpetrators to justice. Law and order are essential to the well-being of any community and every honest citizen believes in their enforcement.

But the union spy is not in business to protect the community. He has little respect for law, civil or moral. Men of character do not engage in such work and it follows that the men who do are, as a rule, devoid of principle and ready to go to almost any extreme to please those who employ them.

At the bottom of the whole system of espionage in labor unions, is the one word, GRAFT. The individual operative grafts on the detective agency employing him and the agency grafts on the corporation which pays the bills. In neither case is there honest value received for the money that is paid. The system is an incentive to the commission of crime.

In the structural ironworkers' organization, the spy system flourished for a number of years. Officials of the American Bridge Company and of the National Erectors' Association say the system has been discontinued, at least so far as the employment of private detective agencies are concerned. The Erectors' Association still employs some detectives directly, but they are openly known as such and, of course, are not members of the union.

In the early years of the open shop fight, Mr. Drew of the Erectors' Association says he engaged the Thiel Detective Agency, the Corporations' Auxiliary Company and some others. Mr. Drew "supposes" that these agencies placed their men in the different local unions of ironworkers. The acts of violence that were being committed at the time, he thinks, warranted the employment of such spies.

How far some of these spies were themselves responsible for acts of violence, is difficult to determine, because the spies were unknown except in a very few instances. Where they were known they were expelled from the union, after being given a trial. One man named Berry was expelled from the New York local in 1908 and is now said to be the active head of an independent union of ironworkers in St. Louis. Another man named Darling was expelled from the Hartford, Conn., local in 1910. A man named Blake was admitted to the Philadelphia local, but disappeared when he was suspected of being a spy.

In the spring of 1906, a man named Guthrie was admitted to the New Jersey local. A short time afterward, with two other members of the union he was arrested carrying dynamite into a building being erected by Post & McCord at Twenty-second street and Second avenue in New York City. He was released on bonds, said to have been furnished by a member of the Iron League Employers' Association. The other men pleaded guilty and were sent to prison. Guthrie disappeared. The suspicion among the union ironworkers at the time was that Guthrie was a spy, who planned the explosion and informed his employers when the attempt was to be made, so that the arrests followed. Of course, he found willing accomplices, or it would not have been possible for him to go as far with the plan as he did. But if he suggested it, as charged by the union officers, he was more guilty than the willing tools who assisted him in his plans.

While the identity of the spies became known in the unions in only rare instances, suspicion pervaded every local. Dozens of men were suspected although sufficient evidence against them could not be found to warrant bringing them to trial. The effect was utterly demoralizing on the unions. Honest men were deterred from expressing their views on questions of policy, because of the fear that they might be considered agents of the employers. Men mistrusted each other, as they did their officers. There is nothing quite as repugnant to the honest union man as the idea of being thought a spy.

Mr. Ryan had a reputation among his fellows of being incorruptible. When he went to Pittsburgh, after the last conference held with officials of the American Bridge Company, and urged the local to waive its claim to the erection of the McKeesport tube mill so that a settlement could be reached, it can be readily understood how he felt when he was accused of trying to "sell out." Had he taken advantage of his authority and made a settlement in spite of the Pittsburgh local which he might have done, he would have saved himself and the organization many subsequent troubles, but he might never have been able to overcome the suspicion that he had "sold out." And the American Bridge Company was to a large extent responsible for creating that feeling of suspicion in the minds of the union ironworkers.

In 1903, when Mr. Buchanan was president of the ironworkers' organization, he had occasion to see something of the espionage system. During the national strike in March of that year, Mr. Buchanan had no fewer than eight of these spies on his staff at one time. Eight men, drawing pay from the American Bridge Company and other iron erectors, secretly were reporting to Mr. Buchanan. In fact, he frequently wrote the reports which they sent to their employers.

If there were eight at one time who were "double-crossing" their employers, it is reasonable to assume that there were a number who were not. It gives some idea of the extent of the system even at that time, when the employers and the unions were working under contractual relations.

The American Bridge Company at that time and afterward, maintained an agency in the Frick Building in Pittsburgh under the charge of a man named Thomas H. Morgan. Mr. Buchanan in 1903 bribed a clerk in Mr. Morgan's office and obtained a list of members of the union who were supposed to be on the payroll of the company as secret spies. The list contained twenty-five or more names, among them being the names of some prominent officers of local unions. There were names of men on the list of whom Mr. Buchanan was suspicious but there also were a few names of men in whom he had the utmost confidence. That fact made him attach little importance to the list. He came to the conclusion that Mr. Morgan was carrying a padded payroll, or that the bribed clerk had given him a fictitious list.

That union spies were active in the affairs of the ironworkers' organization at that period, there appears little doubt. It appeared to be the business of Mr. Morgan and other agents not only to keep watch on union affairs, but to endeavor to control union elections. That money was furnished by employers to control delegates to the international convention in Kansas City in 1903, is commonly believed among union ironworkers.

It was at the Kansas City convention that Mr. Buchanan waged a fight against Sam Parks of New York and won by a close margin. In New York stories are told of the amount of money spent among delegates to bring about Mr. Buchanan's re-election. In Pittsburgh and other cities, stories are told of the money spent to defeat Mr. Buchanan.

The first thought that comes on hearing such stories eleven years later is that they are untrue. It would not appear reasonable that employers were using money to defeat Mr. Buchanan and also to re-elect him.

Careful study of the peculiar conditions existing in the trade at that time, however, tends to confirm the stories. It is quite probable that money was used to influence votes both for and against Mr. Buchanan.

In New York the employers were making a desperate fight against Sam Parks. The ironworkers were locked out for having rejected the Arbitration Plan of the Building Trades' Employers' Association. A new independent union had been formed and Mr. Buchanan favored the union as a means through which to eliminate Parks and the methods for which he stood. It is not only possible, but highly probable that the New York employers were willing to pay for the elimination of Parkism. This would explain why some delegates who attended that convention from the Parks faction, state positively that money was used to influence votes for Mr. Buchanan. It does not follow that Mr. Buchanan knew anything about it.

On the other side of the question stands the fact that Mr. Buchanan had that year conducted a successful fight against the American Bridge Company and the Erectors' Association and had forced them into signing a national agreement. It is not unreasonable therefore, to suppose that they might have preferred to see another man at the head of the organization.

Mr. Morgan of Pittsburgh is credited with having been the
disbursing agent on that side.

It is of little importance now how the money was used in
that convention. It is mentioned to show that employers were
greatly interested in the control of the ironworkers' organization, which was no more a part of their business than it would
have been the business of the union ironworkers to try and
control an election in the National Erectors' Association.

It was all a part of the espionage system to control the
union and destroy its effectiveness. It is probable that the
extent of this attempted control was greatly exaggerated in
the minds of the union ironworkers. The effect on their
minds would have been the same whether there actually were
spies in every local union or whether they only suspected it.
It aroused in them a feeling of bitter antagonism against the
firms opposing them, that made reprisals natural, if not inevitable. The ironworkers felt that the existence of their
union was being threatened from without and within. That
did not justify the resort to physical violence and the destruction of property which marked the fight against the open shop,
but it suggests an explanation for the attitude of mind which
made such acts possible.

In a report to the Philadelphia convention in 1905 Mr. Buchanan said on the subject of spies in the union:

"Sadly enough I find in many of our affiliated locals some
persons who are traitors to their cause. These people, however, are generally of the same type and are easily detected
by those who use discrimination and judgment. They are
people who take the side of the employer in nearly every case
and when occasion demands, they charge dishonesty to those
who support efforts to win, whether they are members of the
rank and file, the local officers or the national officers.

"You must watch these people if you would, not that they
get the upper hand. They are regular in their attendance at
the meetings; they are prompt to take the floor in defense of
their masters; they talk louder and longer than any one else.
They do their work in the meetings; they talk it upon the jobs,

before the labor union convenes, after some of the members
have gone home and by sheer physical force even drive persons to support their claim.

"You must watch these people if you would not that they
be thrown out; their advice should not be taken. 'A house
divided against itself cannot stand,' and if these people are
allowed to have their way, you as a labor organization might
as well disband. It cannot win a fight. It cannot make good
the promises it makes its membership and it is a useless thing,
not because the employers are too strong, but because the
stealthy, scheming traitors to the cause are too numerous and
too successful."[1]

It is evident that the men Mr. Buchanan had in mind were
those who openly espoused the cause of the employers and
sought to discredit the local and national officers. Such men,
however, are not the most dangerous in a union. The spy
who is on the payroll of a detective agency, usually is loud
in his denunciation of the employers. He aims at being among
the most radical, so that he may be elected to some important
office. If he openly sided with the employers he would not
be apt to get elected. So he pursues a different line of policy
for the purpose of getting elected and at the same time ward-
ing off suspicion as to his real purpose. Once elected to an
important position he is much more valuable to his employer
and can better betray the men he was elected to represent.

In the Dynamite Conspiracy trials in Indianapolis, it was
shown by testimony that H. S. Hockin, a member of the Executive Board of the International Association of Bridge and
Structural Ironworkers, and the man who for three years directed the dynamite campaign in the destruction of bridges
and buildings, was keeping L. L. Jewel, erecting manager for
the McClintic-Marshall Construction Company, and later Detective Burns, informed of the movements of the dynamiters.
Had he not occupied a position of influence in the organization,
that would not have been possible.

1—Convention Report, Bridgemen's Magazine, October 1905.

The evidence in the trial does not show that Hockin became "conscience-stricken" until July, 1910, after he had been found out grafting on Ortie McManigal, by "holding out" from $50 to $75 on each job dynamited by the latter. This had been going on for about three years before the discovery was made. Within two weeks after Hockin's dishonesty was found out, he went to Mr. Jewell and informed him about the work of destruction.[1]

Two months later, in September, 1910, Hockin informed Detective Raymond Burns of the identity of McMänigal and J. B. McNamara.

While there is nothing in the testimony to show that Hockin had any connection with the employers or detectives until the summer of 1910, there is a strong suspicion in the minds of some union officials that he was a spy from the first and succeeded in getting elected on the Executive Board to better enable him to carry on the work of destruction.

In opposition to this theory is the fact that Hockin directed the work of dynamiting for three years without the perpetrators being discovered. Had he been in the employ of the erectors during that time, it would appear unlikely that the campaign of destruction could have been carried on successfully so long.

The facts in the case, however, are that McManigal and J. B. McNamara caused some ten explosions after their identity was known to Detective Burns and during the time they were being "shadowed." From that it does not appear that it always is the work of detectives to prevent the commission of crime.

1—Testimony of Mr. Jewell p. 2675-2690, Vol. 3 Transcript of Record, U. S. Circuit Court of Appeals.

CHAPTER XVI.

LABOR VIOLENCE AND THE PUBLIC ATTITUDE.

No phase of the industrial problem attracts quite as much public attention as a resort to physical force during strikes and lockouts. There is more misrepresentation and downright hypocrisy in connection with violence in industrial disputes, than there is with any other phase of this tremendously human problem.

It is natural that the subject of violence should attract more public attention than any other phase of an industrial dispute, although it is only incidental. Fundamental questions like the right to bargain collectively; the right to receive a fair living wage; the right to healthful sanitary conditions; the right to have some leisure time for rest and recreation, are all vitally important to the workers engaged in a strike, but they fail to attract the attention of those not directly interesed.

That indefinite factor, known as the public, is never greatly interested in a strike or industrial war, unless it directly feels the pressure. If the strike affects the supply of some article of daily consumption, or inconveniences the public with respect to food, fuel or transportation, then the public takes an interest in the struggle.

Even in such cases, the chief interest of the public is to have peace; peace at any price, so that it may not be inconvenienced. The public has a rather smug conscience and is less interested in seeing that justice is done in a labor dispute, than that it may have its daily wants and comforts supplied without trouble or inconvenience.

When a strike is of such proportions as to affect the convenience of the public, or is attended with a great deal of violence, the public may then begin to take sides with the actual participants in the struggle. In such cases the result usually is blind partisanship, without regard to the merits of the controversy.

There can not be an educated public opinion without knowledge of the exact facts and it is impossible for the public, as such, to obtain the necessary first hand information. It is seldom that an official body makes a complete investigation of an industrial conflict and publishes its findings for the guidance of the public, at a time when such findings would be of value.

If public opinion, which has proved a powerful influence in other directions, is to be used to further justice in industrial disputes, some machinery should be created to make that public opinion an educated one. If public opinion is not formed on a knowledge of the facts, it is worse than useless, because it tends only to stir up class prejudice and intensify the struggle.

Acts of violence, committed during strikes, have greater influence on public opinion than the fundamental issues. As these acts of violence, at least the spectacular ones that reach the eyes and ears of the public, are usually committed by the strikers and their active sympathizers, it follows that public opinion, based on such acts, is adverse to the strikers.

But it may happen, and frequently does, that the employer is guilty of the first act of violence. It is a form of violence that is within the written law; but violence, nevertheless. The violence committed by the strikers usually is a violation of the written law, consequently it is condemned and the participants punished. The violence committed by the employer, which is not a violation of the written law, is overlooked, or never thought of by the public, because attention has not been directed toward it.

It is puerile to contend that force and violence are not accompaniments of strikes and lockouts. In the very nature of things they must be. A strike, or lockout, is simply a method of applying force to attain a certain desired result. It cannot be anything else. In the case of a strike, the workers withdraw their labor power to force an employer to grant certain demands. In a lockout the employer closes his factory to force the employees to accept certain conditions which he desires to impose. It is force either way it is looked at.

In shutting down a factory in order to bring about certain

conditions which he desires, an employer may be guilty of using the most ruthless kind of force. He is within his rights under the written law, consequently he feels justified in holding up his head among his fellows and denouncing acts of violence committed by strikers.

But he is himself guilty of using force. He uses the weapons of hunger and want; thus making helpless women and children—non-participants in the struggle—suffer, so that he may attain his desired ends.

When the door of the factory closes and the employees are paid the wages due them, the employer takes the position that his former workers have no further interest in his factory. The law says he is right in that position. He is not, therefore, violating any written law.

The doors of the factory open a week later and the employer announces that any man or woman, willing to accept the conditions of employment which he has established, may find work in that factory as long as there are positions to be filled. The employer is again within his rights under the law. There is no incentive for him to violate the written law, because the law agrees with him in what he desires to do.

But the workers who were locked out because they refused to accept the conditions imposed, or because they demanded improved conditions, take quite a different view of the situation. They feel they have a property right in the jobs they formerly held. That the law holds they have no such right, and that anyone who is willing to accept the conditions, shall have a right to fill the jobs, without fear of molestation, does not alter the situation in the minds of the workers. They look upon the new employees as enemies, who are taking the bread and butter out of their mouths and the mouths of their families.

They cannot see the justice of the law. It is quite plainly on the side of the employer, at least in the particular instance in which they are vitally interested. They refuse to accept the dictum of the law and of the employer, that they no longer have any claim on their former jobs. They want the jobs,

which they think are theirs. In order that they may get the
jobs, it is necessary to prevent others from taking them. They
cannot go to the employer and ask him not to fill their old
positions. He has already made himself perfectly clear on that
point.

What is the natural thing for the strikers to do? Prevent
new employes from taking the jobs in that factory, of course.
If that can be done by peaceful methods, so much the better.
If it cannot, then it must be done by violent methods. The
important thing is that it be done. That is the way the workers view the situation, the law to the contrary notwithstand-
ing.

The factory is picketed. The courts have held that "peaceful picketing" is not unlawful. It may be lawful, but it is
entirely useless and ineffective. It is not necessary for the
courts to restrain "peaceful picketing" although they sometimes have done it. The only purpose in picketing a factory
is to prevent certain workers taking the places vacated by
certain other workers. The theory of "peaceful picketing"
is, that the workers seeking employment in that particular
factory, will voluntarily turn away when they are told that a
strike or lockout is in progress.

In actual practice they do nothing of the kind, or only in
rare instances. The pickets know that; so do the employers.
It is not necessary that the pickets actually assault the employees who desire to enter the factory. If the pickets as-
semble in sufficient numbers, it is possible to intimidate those
seeking employment, without actually assaulting them. But it
is the fear of possible assault that brings results; not moral
suasion. The "moral suasion" argument is good in the court-
room or on the public platform, but around the factory it
counts for practically nothing. Every one with practical experience of conditions knows that. It is better to meet the
facts squarely than to dodge them by subterfuge and hypocrisy.

In his testimony before the United States Commission on
Industrial Relations, at a public hearing in New York, Vin-

cent St. John, secretary of the Industrial Workers of the World, said that he believed in violence, if it was necessary to win. He said that if the destruction of property seemed necessary to bring results, then he believed in the destruction of property.

In defense of his views he said the employers did not hesitate to destroy the property of the workers, which is their labor power, by forcing them into mills and factories at an early age; by depriving them of the chances to attain an education; by working them long hours so that their health and efficiency became impaired and their labor power, which is their property, destroyed.

The views of Mr. St. John are extreme and most labor leaders will openly repudiate them. But there is no denying the fact that Mr. St. John gave public expression to views that are privately entertained by tens of thousands. It is *results* that the workers are striving for and the history of the labor movement proves that they have been compelled to fight for every important improvement in conditions which they now enjoy.

It is true that fighting does not necessarily mean resort to physical violence. The workers have made marked progress through legislation, but in that field, as in the industrial field, they have had to meet and overcome the same determined opposition.

The railroads of the country for years fought against the introduction of automatic couplers and other safety devices intended to protect the lives and limbs of the workers. Employers generally have fought against every effort to reduce hours of labor by legislation. They have opposed measures intended to protect health and life in mines, mills and factories.

There are some conditions, however, that cannot be improved by legislative enactment. The question of physical violence and violation of law, is therefore largely one of local conditions. As the laws are mainly designed to protect property rights, with little regard for human rights, it is inevitable that in fighting for the latter, the law will at times be violated.

In the case of the lockout in the factory referred to, it might be possible for the workers to keep strictly within the law. They might submit to the conditions which the employer imposed, or they might quietly go about their business and find employment elsewhere, if they could. That is what the employer and what the law says they must do. But it is not human nature to do it. It is not the way of progress. Had the workers always taken the course which the letter of the law requires them to take, they would, in all probability still be working twelve or fourteen hours a day.

There are different forms in which force may be applied. It may be applied without any violation of the written law. The form of application depends on the peculiar conditions in the situation and the training and environment of the person applying the force.

If it is a banker, business or professional man, who seeks to obtain an advantage over a competitor, he will resort to methods that are not definitely prescribed by law. He may impair the credit of his competitor so that he cannot borrow capital necessary in his business. He may undersell him in the market and force him to the wall. He may adopt a dozen different methods to attain his end.

If it is a hodcarrier, or a structural ironworker who is applying the force, the method used will be entirely different. The hodcarrier sees a competitor who is underselling him and his first natural impulse is to "punch the head" of that competitor. He follows the impulse, too, if there is no policeman in sight. The finesse of the professional man is unknown to the hodcarrier. He does the thing that is natural for a man of his training to do to obtain the advantage he desires.

The underlying motive of the hodcarrier, however, is the same as that of the professional man. He is aiming to advance his material interests and he takes what seems to him the most direct route to that end.

So it runs through our whole business and social life. Force is everywhere apparent, differing only in degree and method of application. The nature of the force is determined by the immediate environment of the person applying it. It may be legitimate, that is, within the written law, or it may be otherwise according to circumstances. But it is there.

Force always has been used when it seemed necessary to attain the object sought A baby will kick and scratch to obtain possession of a prized toy. It is a natural instinct which centuries of civilization and culture have been unable to eradicate.

The use of force may be a symptom of savagery or of strength and virility, according to the point of view and the object for which it is invoked. In legalized warfare the man who fights and maims his fellows, is hailed as a hero. In an industrial war the man who maims an opponent is termed a "thug." Monuments are erected to the memory of one and prison doors yawn open to receive the other. In both instances violence is committed. And the law of property rights makes the difference.

CHAPTER XVII.

THE DEVELOPMENT OF THE PROFESSIONAL SLUGGER.

The use of force and violence to attain a desired end, is a common attribute of mankind. It did not originate with labor unions. Neither are they the only agencies which practice it. The industrial history of the last few years shows that some of the most violent strikes have been among unorganized workers.

When such revolts occur among unorganized workers, violence and disorder are always more pronounced than where there is an organization, for the reason that there is no restraining influence among the strikers. Organization implies order and system and every observer of industrial disputes knows, that the more perfect the organization, the less violence accompanies a strike.

The explanation of that fact is, of course, simple. It is not the mere act of striking that produces violence. The violence begins when the employers attempt to resume work with non-union employes. If a trade is almost perfectly organized, the employers seldom attempt to resume operations, hence there can be no violence, because there is no occasion for it. But the organization of the workers also has a tendency to minimize violence, because of the better discipline which it produces and the confidence it gives the strikers in their ability to secure justice without a resort to physical force.

In 1910 more than 50,000 coal miners in Illinois were on strike for six months and no violence was committed. In fact there were fewer breaches of the peace in the mining sections of the state during the strike, than was usual in normal times. The strikers had less money to spend in saloons, consequently there were fewer personal brawls.

In Colorado in 1913-14 with one-fifth of the number of miners involved, there was a reign of violence and lawlessness that shocked the country. Yet the coal miners in Colorado are much the same kind of men as the coal miners in Illinois. It was the attitude of the coal operators and local conditions which produced opposite results.

In Illinois no attempt was made to operate the mines with non-union men. There was consequently no need to employ mine guards and other agencies that tend to disturb the peace. Both sides were content to make the contest one of endurance.

In Colorado the operators assumed an entirely different position. They would not even discuss conditions with the representatives of the miners. They determined to operate the mines in the way it pleased themselves. Violence was met with greater violence and the result was bloodshed and murder.

Comparison of the two strikes mentioned, shows that organization of labor is not primarily responsible for violence. The Illinois miners were much better organized than were the Colorado miners. The analogy tends rather to show that perfect organization eliminates or minimizes violence, because it removes the immediate cause, which is the unorganized worker.

It has been said that there are different methods of applying force to attain a desired result, some within the written law and some that are not. So there are different forms and degrees of violence in connection with labor disputes.

The impulse to "punch the head" of a man who takes a job which another man feels belongs to him, although he has no legal right to it, is a natural impulse. The average mind cannot conceive of such an act being a heinous crime. But it is the beginning which frequently leads to heinous crimes.

Violence grows. From "punching the nose of a scab" openly, where he has a chance to strike back, it is only a few steps to lying in ambush for him and trying to brain him with a bludgeon.

In recent years there has been a marked change in the nature of the violence committed in the building trades and in the methods used. The ordinary workman who in former days was apt to use his fists on the head of a "scab" for the sake of "the cause", seldom does so now. His place has been taken by the professional thug and gunman. Violence has become commercialized and made more brutal. Assaults on non-union workmen are seldom made openly as in former days when the strikers did the assaulting. The professional slugger lies in wait for his victim, assaults him with a bludgeon or probably shoots him to death.

There are several reasons for this change for the ordinary assault with fists, committed on the impulse of the moment by the otherwise law-abiding workman, to the murderous, brutal assault committed by the hired thug. Employers have organized into associations in their respective lines of business. Through these associations they have been able to give publicity to acts of lawlessness and arouse public sentiment. They have stirred up public officials and aided in the detection and punishment of offenders. They have invoked the aid of the courts and obtained injunctions making punishment more certain and more drastic.

These repressive measures have made open assaults on non-union workmen by crowds of strikers dangerous in large cities. So the professional slugger has been developed. It is not necessary that he be a member of the union for which he does the slugging. He may not be a member of any union; oftentimes he is not. He is not interested in "the cause." He is ready to commit any kind of crime for pay. He may be employed in a gambler's war one day; in a labor war the next and the following day involved in a political row. He will slug for either side in a contest if he is paid his price.

If the destruction of property seems more expedient than the slugging of non-union men, the professional will attend to that. It makes no difference to him what the crime, or who hires him to commit it.

These professional gunmen and sluggers are to be found in every large city. They usually work under a leader of their own choosing. The agent who employs them does business with the leader of the gang. He tells him the nature of the "work" he wants done and the price he will pay. The leader attends to the details. When the crime has been committed, the agent who hired the professional may, with some degree of truth, say he does not know who committed it. He does not know who did the actual "work" and he does not care to inquire.

That such a system of organized thuggery obtains in many of the building trades unions is beyond dispute. The rank and file of the unions do not know anything about it, for obvious reasons. The agent who has the "work" done is himself frequently in ignorance of the identity of the actual perpetrators. That being the case, it would be absurd to suppose that the rank and file of the union know.

"Do you approve of violence in labor disputes?" was the question put to an old member of a building trades union in Chicago, who has been active in union affairs for a quarter of a century.

"Did we ever get anything in the early days without violence?" he asked in reply. "But," he added, "I don't believe in the professional sluggers who are employed today. A bunch of murdering, blackmailing crooks. I wouldn't have them around me and I protest every time an appropriation is made for 'organizing purposes.'

"Punch a scab? Why that is all right. I have done that and we never thought of pay for it. Of course it isn't so necessary today with the perfect organization we have, but there isn't the same spirit in the boys now. We used to go out and clean up a job and the union didn't even allow us car fare. Now the professional bums and blackmailers wouldn't cross the street to hit a scab unless they are assured of their pay. I don't believe in that kind of violence."

This is the point of view of a man much above the average in intelligence. It shows the distinction which the union man makes between "punching a scab" for the good of "the cause" and the professional thuggery that has been developed in recent years. It shows the difference between fighting for what is conceived to be a principle and fighting for hire. The law, of course, cannot make any such fine distinction. Neither does it alleviate the pain and suffering of the victim, to know that he was slugged "for principle" rather than for pay.

In giving his views on the subject of violence, the union man quoted above told an interesting story of what he said was the first organized, systematic violence in connection with building trades strikes in Chicago. It was during a strike of carpenters in 1886 for an eight-hour workday. The trade was poorly organized at the time and there were more ten-hour than eight-hour jobs in the city.

The "general" who organized the violence spent a few days studying a map of the city and noting reports brought him of the various jobs under construction and the number of men employed on each. The location of the jobs was marked on the map. When the time came to strike the blow the "general" distributed his forces with care and precision. He wished to avoid physical force if possible, so he arranged it that the invaders in every instance would outnumber the invaded.

The union men who were working on eight-hour jobs did not begin work until 8 o'clock. The non-union men began work at 7 o'clock. The union men who worked in the near vicinity of the non-union jobs were directed to meet on certain street corners at 7 o'clock next morning. The orders of the "general" were obeyed to the letter and at precisely the same minute, dozens of non-union jobs were "cleaned out" in different sections of the city. The union men who did the "cleaning" were all at their own jobs ready for work at 8 o'clock, so they had good alibis if necessary.

"And it worked to perfection," said the man telling the story. "It struck terror to the hearts of the scabs and the bosses at the same time. They didn't know when the lighting might strike again. And there was little actual violence. Most of the scabs ran when we entered the buildings and not a man was arrested. The scabs joined the union in hundreds in the next few days. That was the first organized violence in the building trades in Chicago and it won for us. Of course, I believe in violence of that kind when it is necessary to win."

Such were the methods used before slugging was commercialized and made a business for professionals.

Not all the violence in connection with strikes, however, is committed by professionals. Should a general strike in a trade take place in a city and the employers attempted to resume with non-union men, the strikers would be apt to try and prevent it and clashes would follow. In the building trades, however, which are well organized, general strikes in a trade are unusual. Because of the thorough organization; the necessity for proceeding with certain jobs and the ease with which the contractor can shift the added cost on to the owner, there are some who are always ready to meet the union demands.

Most of the building trades strikes in recent years have been directed against individual employers on particular buildings. The number of men involved on any particular job is comparatively small, so that a few professional sluggers can take care of the situation. There is less danger in the professional getting caught, as his experience enables him to elude the police.

Many statements are made that labor unions do not believe in violence. If the statements mean that the average union man would not himself commit violence, they are true. If they mean that the average union man, in the building trades, does not approve of violence, if it brings the results sought, then the statements are not true. The average building trades mechanic is interested in results and he is not apt to inquire closely into the methods used, if the results are attained. The fact that he has no personal knowledge of acts of violence, relieves his mind of responsibility.

Ask the ordinary union man in any building trade if he approves of violence and he probably will answer that he does not. He would not think of assaulting a non-union man himself. He would not destroy property under any circumstances.

If he hears or reads, however, of a building that is being erected by non-union men in his particular craft, having been destroyed by dynamite and that the employer as a result has decided to employ union men, he does not feel overwhelmed with grief over the outrage.

If he attends a meeting of his union and hears a veiled report that an "accident" happened on a certain job the other day and that the omployer has since signed an agreement with the union, he will nudge his companion and whisper "good work." He may add, "of course, I don't believe in that sort of thing, but it seems to bring results." And his companion will reply that the business agent is "all right" and both will vote for his re-election.

CHAPTER XVIII.

The Dynamite Campaign and Its Effect.

The arrests April 12, 1911, of Ortie E. McManigal and J. B. McNamara, the self-confessed agents of the structural ironworkers in the destruction of property by explosives, and the arrest ten days later of J. J. McNamara, secretary of the International Association of Bridge and Structural Ironworkers as the directing head of the alleged dynamiters, threw the country into a form of national hysteria. The importance of the arrests was magnified out of all proportion with their actual bearing on the industrial situation.

This was largely a result of the spectacular and sensational manner in which the arrests were made; the confession of McManigal; the way in which J. J. McNamara was taken out of the State of Indiana in violation of the established legal procedure in such cases and the desire for publicity and notoriety on the part of the private detectives employed by the National Erectors' Association, who made the arrests.

Overshadowing every crime with which the alleged dynamiters were charged, was the destruction of the Los Angeles Times Building on October 1, 1910, through which twenty-one persons lost their lives. Through carefully planned publicity, the destruction of the Times Building was skillfully coupled up with the destruction of numerous bridges and buildings throughout the country, and in the public mind, the structural ironworkers were charged with the entire responsibility.

The International Association of Bridge and Structural Ironworkers, as an organization, had nothing to do with the Times explosion. J. B. McNamara pleaded guilty to having caused the explosion and he was, according to the evidence adduced in the Dynamite Conspiracy Trials, the same agent who caused numerous explosions on buildings and bridges for the structural ironworkers. That is the only connection between the structural ironworkers and the Times explosion.

While the same agent was employed, because of his expert

knowledge of explosives, it does not follow that his employers were the same. Who did employ McNamara to blow up the Los Angeles Times has never been determined. No one except McNamara himself has been tried or convicted of the crime. The Times explosion, therefore, must be considered separate and apart from the hundred other explosions and attempted explosions on buildings and bridges throughout the country.

Without in any way attempting to minimize the enormity of the crime which cost the lives of twenty-one human beings, it may be said on the most reliable authority, that it was not the intention of McNamara to take human life. The charge of dynamite used, was not of itself sufficient to wreck the entire building. The explosion did not stop the running of the presses.

According to the authority of Mr. Clarence S. Darrow, who defended the McNamara brothers and who knows the facts better, perhaps, than anyone else except McNamara himself, what actually happened was this: The charge of dynamite was placed near a number of barrels of printer's ink, which contains petroleum in large quantities and is highly inflammable. The force of the explosion burst the ink barrels and scattered the flaming fluid all around. The building was a firetrap and the flames spread so rapidly that the men at work had no chance to escape. They were suffocated or burned to death.

While McNamara could not foresee the results of his work, he, of course, took chances and it does not greatly mitigate his crime to say that he did not intend to take human life. Although he was a zealot, ready to do anything in his blind devotion to a cause, as he conceived it, he must have realized the grave possibilities of his act, if he was capable of reasoning at all.

Aside from the Los Angeles Times explosion, for which the structural ironworkers were not responsible, no loss of life attended any of the other explosions, extending over six years that the dynamite campaign covered in the war against the open shop in the structural iron industry. The destruction of property was not as great as commonly supposed, for the reason that buildings under construction are open and are not susceptible to serious damage from an explosion.

While the estimated loss caused by a few of the explosions ran into thousands of dollars, the average loss probably did not exceed $1,000 for each explosion. Some of the larger structural iron firms carried dynamite insurance and the cost of the premiums was added to the contract price, so that in many instances there was little financial loss to the erectors.

They were, of course, compelled to employ additional watchmen and in other ways subjected to inconveniences and delays that were costly, but in dollars and cents the dynamite campaign appears to have cost the union more than it did the employers.

According to the testimony of McManigal, who turned state's evidence, and the union records introduced in evidence during the trial of the officers of the ironworkers organization in Indianapolis, the price paid by the union for each explosion was $200 and expenses.

From February, 1908, to April, 1911, 70 explosions took place; 43 on jobs of members of the National Erectors' Association and 27 on work of independent contractors.[1] Of the known explosions McManigal was the agent in twenty cases and J. B. McNamara in sixteen cases. In all about one hundred explosions, or attempts to dynamite, occurred from the beginning of the year 1906 until the end of the year 1911.

The Dynamite Conspiracy Trials, as a result of which twenty-two former officials of the ironworkers' union, in addition to the McNamara brothers, are now serving sentences in a federal prison, cost the organization at least $150,000 as shown by the records, independent of what the ironworkers contributed to the defense of the McNamara brothers. If to this sum is added the price paid to the actual agents who wrought the work of destruction, together with their expenses,

---

1—U. S. Brief, p. 27, U. S. Circuit Court of Appeals, Dynamite Conspiracy Cases.

it will be seen that the average cost to the union of each explosion was about $2,000, or twice the estimated cost to the employers. In addition the union is continuing to pay $25 a week to each of the men in prison, except H. S. Hockin, so that from a financial point of view the dynamite campaign must be considered a failure for the union.

Did the campaign pay in other respects? What effect did it have on the growth and financial standing of the organization? What effect on the smaller contractors who were not in a position financially to assume risks?

In a previous chapter it has been shown that the National Erectors' Association is today in a stronger position than it ever occupied. Its membership controls a larger proportion of the steel erection work than it did when the fight began. Its force of open shop workers are more efficient due to their greater experience. As some of its members were protected against financial loss through dynamite insurance, it is reasonable to assume that the campaign of destruction might have been continued indefinitely without causing a change of the attitude of the Erectors' Association. On the contrary the dynamite outrages increased the determination of members of the Erectors' Association not to have any further dealings with the union.

Toward the end of the year 1911 negotiations were opened between the Employers' Association of Architectural Iron-workers of New York and the union, looking toward the making of a contract. The employers seemed willing to enter into a union agreement with the finishers, or architectural ironworkers, but were prevented from doing so by the Board of Governors of the Building Trades Employers' Association. The reason given was the revelations in connection with the pleas of guilty of the McNamara brothers. As the members of the Employers Association of Architectural Ironworkers were under bonds of $1,000 each, not to make an agreement with a union without the approval of the Building Trades Employers' Association, the negotiations were dropped.[1]

1—Report of J. E. McClory to Indianapolis Convention, February, 1913.

It is an open secret that the finishers, or architectural iron-workers in New York, could today secure a union agreement with their employers if they would sever their affiliation with the International Association. They are being punished because of their affiliation in the same national organization with the structural ironworkers and the dynamite outrages are given as the excuse for refusing to recognize the latter.

These facts point to the conclusion that the dynamite campaign was ineffective so far as it was directed against the National Erectors' Association and that it weakened the influence of the organization with some independent employers.

On the other side, while the campaign of violence was in force, many small employers who feared that their work might be destroyed made agreements with the union. Since the explosions stopped with the arrest and conviction of the conspirators, many of these smaller employers have declared for the open shop. It is this condition which a prominent union official had in mind when he said: "The mistake was not in using dynamite, but in getting caught at it. Had we been able to keep it up we would have won. It kept the little fellows in line and since it stopped they have gone over to the big fellows."

This view is not shared by many of the union ironworkers, most of whom say that the entire campaign was a serious mistake, which cost the organization a great amount of money and loss of prestige, with few compensating returns. An occasional job here and there was unionized, following an explosion in the immediate vicinity, but on the whole dynamite as an organizing force failed to accomplish the main purpose for which it was intended.

While the dynamite campaign does not appear to have had much effect on the big open shop employers, except to intensify the feeling of bitterness toward the union, it does seem to have had a beneficial effect on the numerical strength and financial standing of the organization.

When the open shop fight began the paid up membership of the International Association of Bridge and Structural

Ironworkers was 9,776. This was the membership reported in the Philadelphia convention in September, 1905. The same report showed a treasury balance of $1,013.64. Several death claims and other obligations were unpaid at the time the report was made, so that the organization in reality was in debt at the beginning of the strike.

At the Peoria convention in September, 1914, the report of the secretary-treasurer showed a paid-up membership of 13,184 and a treasury balance of $117,439.25. The membership and treasury balance year by year since the strike began, is shown in the following table:

Year.	Membership.	Treasury Balance.
1904-5	10,216	$1,013.64
1905-6	9,776	6,305.35
1906-7	11,574	15,849.39
1907-8	10,422	18,159.64
1908-9	9,607	24,689.03
1909-10	10,872	34,229.67
1910-11	12,230	51,191.09
1911-12	10,928	101,052.03
1912-13	12,222	107,586.41
1913-14	13,184	117,439.35

The increase in membership may be accounted for by the formation of new locals in some small cities, not organized in 1905 and by the inclusion of locals of machinery movers, pile-drivers and shop men, so that it has no particular significance. It does not denote that the organization controls a larger proportion of structural steel erection work than it did in 1905. On the contrary, while it is not possible to estimate accurately, because the structural steel business fluctuates so much, every indication is that the union controls a smaller percentage of the trade than it did at the beginning of the strike. There has been no appreciable increase in membership of the local unions in any of the large cities, while there has been a decided falling off in some eastern cities where open shop conditions prevail.

The substitution of reinforced concrete for steel in recent years has prevented any remarkable increase in the volume of output of structural steel. The tonnage of the American Bridge Company for 1907 was greater than that of any subsequent year until 1913, and as this company manufactures at least 35 per cent of the total output of the country, the figures may be taken as fairly indicative of the industry as a whole.

It is doubtful, therefore, whether the apparent increase in membership of the ironworkers' organization, as shown on the face of the reports, is due to the dynamite campaign, or in spite of it. Careful analysis of the facts indicates that the latter theory is the correct one.

The remarkable increase in the treasury balance, however, cannot be explained on any other basis than that the membership approved of the campaign and willingly contributed to support it. The members believed that the open shop fight directed against the union, was, in fact a war of extermination and their loyalty was such that they were ready to meet every assessment levied without protest.

This is a condition which obtains in every labor union. In times of peace it is often difficult to collect ordinary dues and a suggestion of a special assessment would result in a protest that the executive officers would have to explain to the satisfaction of the membership. When the same union is engaged in a fight with its employers, it is an easy matter to collect dues and assessments. Opposition brings out the latent fighting qualities in a union as in an individual. It infuses into it new blood and dispels the lassitude which frequently appears after a long period of peace.

No union can stand still and hope to hold its membership. It must advance, either by peaceful methods, or by fighting. If it advances rapidly without much opposition, it is apt to develop a false notion of its own strength and importance, which frequently leads to abuse of power. For that reason the union that has had to fight for every concession gained is likely to be much more conservative and much more stable than the union that has had smooth sailing.

The structural ironworkers are no exception to the rule. In the early years of their organization they had strikes, but most of them were won easily. They had won over the American Bridge Company in local strikes and over the National Erectors' Association in a national strike. They felt that they were invincible and that it was not necessary for them to pay high dues and assessments. The need of a strong defense fund did not appeal to the ironworkers in 1904, which accounts for the fact that the officers at that time were handicapped in their work for lack of funds.

The following table shows the receipts of the national organization for a period of ten years:

Year.	Receipts.
1904-5	$35,580.54
1905-6	50,118.53
1906-7	61,361.60
1907-8	65,956.59
1908-9	54,601.35
1909-10	76,083.70
1910-11	88,577.23
1911-12	150,171.59
1912-13	95,655.07
1913-14	133,612.01

A comparison of the foregoing table with the table on membership, shows that in 1911-12 the membership was only 712 greater than in 1904-5, yet the receipts were more than four times as great, which means that each member contributed about four times as much in the latter year as he did in the former.

It was in the fiscal year 1911-12 that the officers of the International Union were arrested in connection with the dynamiting outrages and the membership loyally supported them by paying heavy special assessments. The comparison proves the truth of the statement that it is when a union meets determined opposition that its treasury swells and that it is difficult to collect dues and assessments when victories come easily.

Another evidence that the campaign of violence had the approval of the membership of the union, is shown by the elections in the national conventions. When Mr. Buchanan was international president from 1901 to 1905, which was undoubtedly the most constructive period in the history of the organization, he had opposition for re-election at every convention. In 1903 he was elected by some two votes and in 1904 he had only four or five votes to spare. In the same period of four years, the office of secretary-treasurer was filled by three different incumbents.

From 1905 until 1913 there was no change in the chief executive officers. Mr. Ryan was re-elected president at each convention, as was Mr. McNamara secretary-treasurer. The latter was re-elected at the Milwaukee convention in 1911 at the time he was in prison in Los Angeles, some two months before he pleaded guilty. Mr. Ryan was re-elected at the Indianapolis convention in 1913 after he had been convicted and while an appeal was pending.

These facts have frequently been pointed to in criticism of the ironworkers' organization. The explanation appears simple enough. Some may still believe that the convicted officials were innocent of the charges, in which case simple justice would demand their re-election. Delegates to a convention probably would know the facts, but would take a different view of the situation from that of the average outsider and therein lies the true explanation.

Assume that the men were guilty as charged and that their conviction was not the result of any "frame-up." They did not plan the destruction of buildings and bridges to further any personal ends of their own. What they did was done in the interests of the organization as a whole. That it may have been a mistaken policy does not alter the situation. It was undertaken in the belief that it would benefit the union. Why then should the union repudiate its own instrument? If the dynamiters had not been caught and if the campaign of violence had won, the leaders would have been regarded as successful generals.

Because they were caught and because the policy did not win, is that a sufficient reason for repudiating them? Would it not be cowardly and morally wrong for the union to step from under and throw the entire blame on the officers? The officers were acting for the union, with at least the tacit approval of the membership. The assessments paid show that. Under the circumstances could the union do less than re-elect the officials? Could it do less than pay their salaries while they are in prison, since they are there for doing what they believed would further the interests of the union?

Had the ironworkers' union disclaimed responsibility for the dynamite campaign and placed the entire blame on the officers by expelling them from membership, it probably would have been commended by some social reformers, but would have been condemned by workingmen generally. Society does not always ostracize the transgressor of moral or civil law. To expect a labor union to do so, especially when the transgressions committed were aimed at furthering the material interests of that union, is to expect something unreasonable.

That is the view the average union man takes of a situation of the kind, whether he is an ironworker or some other mechanic. It may not be a moral view as some would look at it, but there is no cant or hypocrisy about it. The question here is not whether that view is the right one from a moral standpoint, but whether it is the correct one from the ironworkers' point of view.

The National Erectors' Association and other organizations of employers have termed the dynamite conspiracy as "The Crime of the Century." It stirred the public mind as few labor wars have done. The facts are, however, that there have been many other industrial wars that resulted in a much greater loss of life and greater destruction of property.

In the first few years of the open shop fight in the structural iron industry, the assaults on non-union men were numerous and vicious. About one hundred such assaults are recorded and three deaths of watchmen are traced to these attacks. In the dynamite campaign, as has been stated, there was no loss of life or serious injury to any person and the war was prosecuted over a period of more than six years.

In the Colorado coal strike, 74 known deaths occurred in a period of about seven months, before the arrival of the Federal troops on the scene. Measured by the loss of human life the structural ironworkers' fight against the open shop pales into insignificance in comparison with some local strikes which attracted little public attention.

CHAPTER XIX.

WHY THE RESORT TO DYNAMITE?

Destruction of property is not an unusual accompaniment of industrial disputes, the particular form varying according to circumstances. In a dispute between a telephone or telegraph company and linemen, the destruction will consist of cutting wire cables. If between glaziers and their employers, plate glass windows will be smashed. Woodwork sometimes is gouged and defaced in a carpenters' dispute. Whatever the particular form of the vandalism, the object is the same, *i. e.,* to put the employer to additional expense in the hope that he may be compelled to employ union instead of non-union men.

In the case of the structural ironworkers explosives were used because that appeared to be the method which would cause the most destruction. The dynamite bomb had been used in other industrial wars long before the ironworkers adopted it. It was a common weapon in strikes of the Western Federation of Miners in Colorado, Idaho and other western states. It was used extensively in Chicago during a strike against the telephone company, when explosions in underground conduits were common occurrences. It has been used frequently in wars among gamblers and as a means of extorting blackmail, independent of any labor dispute.

The particular agent of destruction used, therefore, has little significance. What is significant is the attitude of mind which justifies such acts and makes the commission of such crimes possible.

As a rule in labor disputes where there is a resort to the destruction of property, it comes only after other methods to obtain the desired results have failed. The first form of violence comes in the shape of attacks on those who take the places vacated by strikers. When that proves ineffective; when the strikers find they cannot prevent the work being done, the next step is to seek to destroy that work.

The underlying motive is the firm conviction in the minds

of the strikers that the particular work belongs to them. They may have refused to perform that work except under conditions acceptable to them. These conditions may not be acceptable to the employer. Still the workers cannot in their minds separate themselves from their jobs and they feel justified in wreaking vengeance both on those who took their places and on the employer who permitted and encouraged it.

With the structural ironworkers, assaults on non-union men marked the beginning of the fight against the open shop. As has been said these assaults were numerous and vicious, but proved wholly ineffective. The number of non-union jobs increased, while the chances of employment of union men decreased. If the non-union men could not be frightened or intimidated because of the assaults, other methods had to be tried.

Assaults on non-union men did not hurt the employer, physically or financially, but if the work was destroyed it might touch him in a vulnerable spot. He would have to stand the financial loss, which might cause him to hesitate before undertaking to erect another building with non-union men.

That is the way the ironworker looked at it. The fact that it was unlawful to destroy property would give him little concern. According to his code of ethics, the "snakes"[1] had no right to take his work. They didn't contribute to the support of the union. They were willing to accept the good wages and conditions which the union had brought about without helping to support it. They were enemies of society in general and of the union ironworkers in particular. They were attempting to break down and destroy certain standards which the union had established. Therefore any means to force them off that work, or into the union, were justifiable, as the union ironworker looked at it.

That the employer had a right to employ non-union men if he chose to do so, would not strike the union ironworker forcibly. He is not concerned about nice points of law or ethics, That the hated "snake" had a right to work; that he probably

---

1—The term applied by union ironworkers to non-union men.

had a family to support; that he was not violating any law by working, would not appeal to the union man. The latter lives daily in a union atmosphere. He does not hear the rights of the employer, or of the non-union man discussed. Only the rights of the union man, or the wrongs, real or fancied, which he has to endure, are topics of conversation in union halls.

It is not to be wondered at, that after years in such an environment, the average union man sees only one side of the question and that is the union side. He loses perspective, if he has ever acquired it.

It is not because he is incapable of reasoning. On the contrary the union school develops remarkably clear thinkers and able reasoners. If their arguments are all directed toward one end, that is only natural. It is well known in the legal profession that a lawyer who has been a prosecuting attorney for years, loses his ability to defend an accused person. He loses mental poise and aims to secure a conviction regardless of the evidence.

If it is true that a prosecuting attorney, with all the advantages that come with education and training, loses mental poise as a result of continuous thought along one groove, it is not to be wondered at that the union man, without such training, develops a biased mental attitude. He can hardly be blamed if he does not see matters from the employer's point of view, even if that point of view may be the correct one. And if employers refuse to meet and discuss working conditions with their employes, how is either going to learn the viewpoint of the other?

To the union man, the union means something more than a machine to maintain fair wages and working conditions. It means an agency for securing employment, if employment is to be had in his particular craft. The union man pays dues into his union for protection. He expects his union to protect him against the competition of the non-union man. If a union man is out of work while a non-union man in his craft is working, then the union man feels he is not receiving the protection for which he is paying. At the bottom of the whole problem lies the dread of unemployment and the competition for jobs.

The union man feels that he should be a preferred customer and have first choice in the matter of obtaining work. If that work must be obtained at the expense of the non-union man, that does not make any difference. It is for that the union man is paying dues. The aim of the union is to have a monopoly of work in a particular trade. It differs from an oppressive monopoly in that any competent workman may join the union and share in the benefits.

Because of that fact, union men are prone to resent an imputation that a union is monopolistic in its tendencies. But it is, nevertheless. In fact the strength or weakness of a union is measured by the extent that it is able to monopolize the work in a particular trade.

By way of illustration, suppose that an open shop firm secures a contract for the erection of a large building or bridge in or near a city where the structural ironworkers are organized. Union men out of work daily see the open shop men at work. They complain to their business agent and at their union meetings. They declare they cannot find jobs while "snakes" are steadily employed right under their noses. They demand to know what they are paying dues for. The business agent realizes that a storm is brewing and he must do something.

One night the bridge or building is wrecked by dynamite. Next day the contractor decides to make a contract with the union. The idle men are given jobs. At the next meeting of the union the business agent may report that the job in question has been "straightened out" and as a result all the idle members have found employment.

Is it reasonable to suppose that the members of the union do not understand why the job was "straightened out?" Is it natural to suppose that they will demand to know of their business agent if he was responsible for the explosion? They wanted to get that work and they got it. They do not know, of course, who caused the explosion. They do not care to inquire. It brought results and that was what they were looking for.

Do they believe in violence? They didn't destroy the property and they don't know who did. They probably adopt resolutions denouncing the unknown perpetrators and offering a reward for their arrest and conviction. The Western Federation of Miners in convention offered a reward for the arrest of the men who blew up the Independence depot in June, 1904, killing fourteen men. Harry Orchard afterward confessed that he and Steve Adams did it, acting as agents for the officers of the union.

In this way do union men collectively approve of violence that few, if any of them, would individually commit. As a matter of principle they believe that violence is wrong. But principle in the abstract has less weight in their minds than the immediate and concrete necessity of finding work. And if violence seems to open the only way leading to a job, then the average building trades workman feels that the end justifies the means.

There is another factor to be considered in the fight of the ironworkers against the open shop. That is the union employer. It would be unjust to charge the union employer with direct responsibility for any of the outrages committed against open shop firms, although unconsciously, he may have been an indirect cause.

In any of the building trades, the contractor who is employing union men complains if a competitor is allowed to go on under non-union conditions. He feels that it is not fair to him to be compelled to live up to union rules and regulations, when his competitors are not subjected to like restrictions. When he is visited by the union business agent because of some minor infraction of a rule, he is apt to get angry and say: "Why don't you go after the non-union work and leave me alone? Mr. Smith and Mr. Jones are employing non-union men. They can underbid me on every job I estimate against them. They are not paying the wages. But you don't bother them. You keep after me. I am growing tired of it and if something is not done soon, I shall quit employing union men."

The argument is logical and the union business agent knows it. If he does not make some effort to stop the non-union work, another firm, probably, will be lost to the union. He is pressed by the members of his union demanding protection from the unfair competition of the non-union man, and he is pressed by the union employer who demands protection against his unfair competitor. Neither suggests violence, but if the non-union firms will not meet the business agent or discuss conditions with him, he resorts to the only expedient which appears open to him. Either the non-union men are assaulted, or an attempt is made to destroy the work.

The structural ironworkers tried both methods and the latter seemed most effective and least dangerous. In the beginning of the trouble, when the slugging of non-union men was the rule, the arrests were numerous and many convictions were obtained. The dynamiters carried on their work of destruction for five years before they were caught.

The main reason for the resort to dynamite is found in the uncompromising attitude of the open shop employers. The American Bridge Company offered to compromise in the early stages of the fight and the union representatives rejected the terms of that compromise. After that the attitude of the employers was unyielding. Every effort on the union side to bring about a conference, after its officers realized the mistake that had been made, proved unavailing.

Without a conference, no settlement of the strike was possible. For the union it meant either unconditional surrender or a fight to a finish. There was no middle course open while the employers refused to confer.

The question here is not whether the American Bridge Company was right or wrong in refusing to hold further conferences after its peace offer was rejected and after attempts had been made to destroy its property. It is a matter of fact that it did refuse.

When the hopelessness of the situation became apparent to

the union officials, resort was made to the destruction of property. Diplomacy was out of the question, so dynamite was tried. It proved to be a colossal blunder, as was the rejection of the peace terms offered in the beginning of the fight.

The campaign of violence was a failure because of the determination and financial resources of the employers opposing the union. Had the ironworkers expended the same money and energy in trying to organize the open shop men by legitimate methods, the results might have been different.

CHAPTER XX.

CONCLUSION.

In a study of conditions obtaining in the structural iron industry and the relations between the ironworkers and their employers, the most striking fact is, that the application of physical force will neither establish nor maintain just and fair relations between employers and employes.

Many instances might be cited in the industrial world, where the use of physical force has, for a time, won advantage for the side that has used it. Such gains, however, are temporary and do not make for permanent industrial peace.

An employer may at times through force of circumstances be compelled to submit to certain conditions which he believes are unjust. Fear of violence and the destruction of property may cause him to make terms with a union against his will and business judgment. But if he is forced to submit through fear or business necessity, he will break from the restraint on the first opportunity.

Workingmen on the other hand may be compelled to submit to conditions which they regard as irksome, if the advantage is on the side of the employer. They submit sullenly, because they are compelled to do so by force of circumstances. Instead of co-operating with their employers under such conditions they are constantly looking for the day when they can turn the tables and get the upper hand.

Force may subjugate one side or the other in an industrial dispute, but it will not remove discontent. It will not establish justice. When one side is all-powerful and the other side is subservient, there is sure to be injustice. Where there is injustice, there will be discontent.

The abuse of power is not always on the side of the employer. Where unions are in complete control, abuses are as apt to develop as where the employers exercise absolute power. In neither case is the condition conducive to industrial peace. Abuses may sometimes be more fancied than real, due to the inability of one side to comprehend the motive of the other side. Frequently it is not the act itself that constitutes the abuse, but the manner in which the act is performed.

If an employer issues an order because he has the power to do so, without regard to the wishes of his employees, the order may be obeyed, but it may create a great deal of dissatisfaction. If a union adopts a certain rule, imposing some restriction on the employer, without his knowledge or consent, the rule may be enforced, but it will arouse the antagonism of the employer. If the union representatives and the employer sat down together and discussed the matter in the light of reason, they would probably agree that the issue was not so important after all.

The aim of a teacher in a public school is to have the pupil perform a certain work without making it appear a task. That would hardly be accompished if the teacher stood over the pupil with a birch rod. The task would be performed, but the pupil would find little pleasure in the work. His good opinion of his teacher would not be enhanced by the performance and the task probably would be poorly performed.

Grownups are not so different from children in that respect. They resent the too free exercise of power over them, unless the reasons for it are explained. The explanation many times will remove the cause of dissatisfaction. It does not meet the situation to say that it is not the business of the employee to reason why, but to obey orders.

In the ironworkers' controversy there was too much of an uncompromising attitude shown on both sides. There was too much of the spirit of wishing to do certain things because of possessing the power to do them.

The ironworkers were the first to display an uncompromising attitude two months after the strike began. The American Bridge Company offered to meet substantially the demands made when the strike was called. It offered to employ union men on all its erection work, whether done by it directly or by sub-contract and to pay the recognized rate of wages.

But the Philadelphia convention of the union added a new

demand, which in substance was that the American Bridge Company should compel the National Tube Company to employ union ironworkers on the erection of a tube mill at McKeesport. The strike was against the American Bridge Company and it was not erecting the tube mill. The union could have accepted the settlement that was offered and won its original demands.

The convention, however, gave emphatic instructions to its officers not to settle until every demand was met. Subsequent events proved that it is unwise for delegates in a convention, who are not in possession of all the facts and details, to outline a policy of conduct for the executive officers in a strike. The officers of the ironworkers' union could not accept a compromise settlement unless they ignored the instructions of the convention.

Later when the union realized the mistake that had been made and was ready to compromise, it was the American Bridge Company that assumed the uncompromising attitude. Its officers refused to hold further conferences with the union representatives. Without a conference, a settlement of the strike was impossible. The union had erred and there was no pardon for it. The company had opened its doors once and invited the union to step in, provided it did not go too far. When it refused the doors were forever barred. It was then that the union, to use a metaphor, tried to blow the doors open with dynamite. They are still closed and barred.

The policy pursued by the ironworkers' organization in the beginning of the strike, in refusing to allow its members to work on sub-contracts, taken by union firms from the American Bridge Company, gave the open shop employers a decided advantage in the contest, an advantage which the union was never afterward able to overcome. This policy was rescinded by the National Executive Board on the advice of President Ryan some eight months after the strike began, but by that time the open shop policy had been firmly established in some localities.

Pursuance of this policy on sub-contracts, led to the open

shop war in New York City and caused the suspension of the ironworkers from the Joint Arbitration Board of the building contractors and building trades unions. This weakened the union by placing it in a position where it did not have the sympathetic support of other trades and in a corresponding degree it strengthened the position of the open shop employers.

The strike on Post & McCord's work in New York, which marked the beginning of the open shop war in that city, cannot be regarded as anything but a violation of a local agreement. There is no conclusive proof that the firm of Post & McCord was directly connected with the American Bridge Company, while on the other hand, the fact that the firm was a party to a local agreement with the ironworkers' union is not disputed. That the international union had authority to order a local on strike, may be admitted. That it was wise or expedient to exercise that authority when the local was under contract with its employers, may be questioned. More especially is this true in the particular instance under consideration, for the reason that the strike on Post & McCord's jobs was called November 1st and the local agreement would have expired by limitation two months later.

Another policy of the ironworkers' union which furnishes one of the chief reasons for the employers desiring to maintain open shop conditions, is its claims of jurisdiction of work. The employers have always desired to employ unskilled laborers at lower pay to perform certain classes of work claimed by the union for its members at the union rate of wages.

Employment of unskilled labor at low wages to do work claimed by skilled labor at higher wages decreases the cost of production. From an economic standpoint that should be encouraged. But here it is difficult to reconcile economic theory with actual practice. Behind the desire of the skilled workman in the building trades to control all the work he can, even when such work might be satisfactorily performed by unskilled labor, lies the question of unemployment.

The dread of unemployment lies at the bottom of most of the

jurisdictional disputes in the building trades. If every skilled workman was assured of steady employment twelve months in the year, he would not feel so jealous if he saw an unskilled laborer, or a skilled workman in another craft, doing work which he believed belonged to the men of his own trade.

The structural ironworker knows from practical experience that he is out of work about one-fourth of the time under normal conditions. It is therefore natural for him to try to extend his trade jurisdiction as much as possible and prevent, if he can, laborers from doing work which he otherwise would have to do. The fight of the unions for closed shop agreements in the building trades, is not entirely one for wages and hours, but also one for control and jurisdiction of work. The more work each union can control, the more work its members believe they will get.

The question of unemployment has a direct bearing also on the question of efficiency and restriction of output. The slogan today is efficiency and scientific management. If there is not enough work now to keep the average building trades workman employed more than nine months in a year in normal times, it is difficult for him to understand why he should increase his efficiency so that he could perform that work in eight months. To him it looks like reasoning from the wrong end, so that the average union man is not wildly enthusiastic over efficiency systems. He is not convinced that he will create new work by increasing his output. As his most pressing problem is to find work, because of an over-supply of labor in his particular trade, he cannot see wherein he is inefficient.

The American Bridge Company and other members of the National Erectors' Association have maintained the open shop because they believe it has been to their financial interests to do so. Under the open shop policy they are free to conduct their operations as best suits themselves. If they desire to employ laborers at a low rate of pay to perform work that under a union agreement would be done by skilled men at higher wages, they do so without fear of strikes. In this way the aggregate wages of the ironworkers are reduced, although the nominal rate per hour for skilled men may be maintained. The fight for the open shop is at bottom a fight for increased profits for the employers.

Comparison of open shop and union wage scales in the structural iron industry, shows that the open shop scale is considerably lower. In New York City, which is on the open shop basis, the wages of ironworkers are lower than in other large cities and have been advanced only once since the fight began in the spring of 1906. As steel erectors who employ union men frequently bid successfully against open shop erectors, it would appear that the economy effected through open shop operation is entirely at the expense of the workmen. If the cost of production is reduced, the consumer does not profit by it.

There is another important, if less direct, reason why the American Bridge Company and other large structural iron firms desire the open shop. They are much less interested in erection work than they are in the manufacture of structural steel in their fabricating shops. They fear the unionizing of their shops much more than they do their erection work. The structural ironworkers' organization claims jurisdiction over the men in the fabricating shops and has made many efforts to organize them, although such efforts have largely been unsuccessful.

The tendency of the U. S. Steel Corporation and its subsidiary companies, has been to prevent the spead of organization among the employes. The tendency of the ironworkers and all other organizations of labor, is, and always has been to extend their sphere of influence. Therein lies the main reason for the clash of interests in this particular situation.

The demand of the structural ironworkers that the McKeesport tube mill be erected by union men, was not in itself very important. It involved the employment of some forty men for a short time. But it was an encroachment of the union in a territory hitherto largely free from union regulations. It might have opened the way for further union aggression.

It is true that the erection of the tube mill had nothing directly to do with the unionizing of the fabricating shops of the American Bridge Company. Had the union been able to force the employment of its members in the new field, however, it would naturally have been encouraged to further efforts in some other direction.

The officials of the U. S. Steel Corporation realized that if the power of the union was to be curbed, the opportune time had arrived. The demand for the erection of the tube mill placed the union in the position of the aggressor. In refusing to accede to the demand, the company took a defensive position.

Later as the fight grew in intensity, the American Bridge Company and some of its associates in the National Erectors' Association became the aggressors, to the extent of insisting that firms taking sub-contracts from them should complete them on the open shop basis. The union, on the other hand used its power and influence to have contracts taken away from open shop firms and frequently it succeeded. Throughout the long campaign, the facts show that the union was on the aggressive and the open shop companies on the defensive.

The erection of the McKeesport tube mill ceased to be an issue early in the fight for the reason that it had been completed. The fight of the union then was to recover the ground that had been lost in the first few months. The fight of the companies was to hold the advantage they had gained. At times an open shop firm made peace with the union. At other times a firm that had been union went over to the open shop side.

Such gains or losses, however, were incidental. The principal firms which declared for the open shop in May, 1906, are still open shop and have been so continuously. If they have suffered the loss of a contract here and there, they have attributed it to the fortunes of war, but such losses have not changed their attitude.

The union has believed throughout that it was in a fight for existence. That in large measure is true. It does not conflict with the statement that the union was on the aggressive and the employers on the defensive. The open shop policy, as understood and practiced by the National Erectors' Association, means the destruction of the union.

Open shop firms will deny that statement and point to the fact that they are employing union men. They are; but not as union men. The open shop erectors do not recognize the right of their employes to bargain collectively. Their employes have no voice in setting wages or working conditions. The employes are simply animated machines who have to do as their employers dictate. They have the privilege of quitting their employment if the conditions do not suit them, which is about the only privilege which the open shop erectors accord their workmen.

As labor unions are organized and exist for the purpose of advancing the material well-being of their members, they cannot exist if deprived of the exercise of their functions in that direction. The policy of the National Erectors' Association prevents the ironworkers' union from exercising the functions for which it was organized. That means the destruction of the union in effect, if not nominally. It means that the union is reduced to a position where it is wholly incapable of protecting the rights of its members. Its existence under such circumstances is a matter of little importance to the employers.

The officers of the ironworkers' union knew what the open shop policy of the erectors actually meant. They knew if that policy succeeded, the union would lose to a like extent. That increased their determination to fight. Denied the opportunity of conferring with representatives of the Erectors' Association, or ending the struggle on the basis of a mutual agreement, they resorted to drastic measures. They found themselves over-matched and, believing the existence of their organization was at stake, they hit below the belt in trying to turn the tide in their favor.

If the union resorted to unfair and unlawful methods in the prosecution of the fight, the erectors were in a degree responsible. The system of espionage which they maintained in local unions, before and after the outbreak of hostilities, did much toward creating and preserving the spirit of hostility which made the destruction of property possible.

It has been shown that the employers maintained a system of espionage in local unions at a time when they were working under contracts with such unions. That does not indicate that they signed the agreements in good faith. If they did sign the agreements in good faith, why was it necessary to keep paid spies in the local unions? Why was it necessary to seek to influence elections in the unions?

That the employers had paid spies in the unions does not admit of doubt. That the system bred suspicion among the members of the union and hatred of their employers, is equally certain. If the employers were not bent on weakening or destroying the influence of the union, at the time they openly recognized it by signing contracts, why the employment of spies?

When the members of the union knew, or suspected, that these paid spies of the employers infested every local, were they not justified in believing that the employers were secretly aiming at the disruption of the union? Is it strange that they should resort to secret methods of retaliation?

Organization raised the wages of structural ironworkers almost 50 per cent in a period of fifteen years. It was natural that they should rally to the support of that union when they believed that its existence was threatened. It was natural that they should feel bitter toward the employers who were hiring secret spies to destroy that union.

The employment of spies by the employers was as indefensible as was the resort to dynamite and the destruction of property by the ironworkers, although the one was within the law and the other was not. The system of espionage was established years before the campaign of destruction began. It cannot, therefore, be urged in defense of the system that it was made necessary because of the outrages that were being committed.

Pernicious as was the effect of the spy system on the union, it did not justify the resort to violence and the destruction of property in the eyes of the law. But it went a long way toward justifying them in the eyes of the union ironworkers.

The employers say that the spy system has been discontinued. It probably has, because under present conditions the open shop erectors are not greatly interested in the union. They feel they have won the fight for the open shop and all they ask of the union is that it leave them alone.

The union ironworkers cannot accept that view. With from 45 to 50 per cent of the structural steel erection on an open shop or non-union basis, it is inevitable that the ironworkers will keep on trying to organize the men in the industry. They look upon the open shop, not only as a check on further progress, but as a menace to the retention of what has already been gained. They feel they must keep on fighting to prevent the spread of the open shop policy, or take a backward step.

Under such conditions there cannot be peace in the industry. Fear of the consequences may prevent a recurrence of violence, but it will not remove the cause. Fear of the law will not reestablish amicable relations between the companies and the union. Only the recognition by each side of the rights of the other can accomplish that, and both sides must agree on what those rights are and define them by mutual consent.

APPENDIX TO REPORT

ON

NATIONAL ERECTORS' ASSOCIATION AND INTERNATIONAL ASSOCIA
TION BRIDGE AND STRUCTURAL IRONWORKERS. CONTAINING
COPIES OF AGREEMENTS AND THE CONSTITUTION AND
BY-LAWS OF THE NATIONAL ERECTORS'
ASSOCIATION.

MEMORANDUM

of

PROPOSED

AGREEMENT

Between the American Bridge
Company .... and the
International Association of
Bridge and Structural Iron
Workers ....

As submitted by the International
Executive Board after hearing the
Report of the Committee representing the Company and the Association.

MEMORANDUM OF CONFERENCE
Held at Pencoyd, Pa.
January 17, 18 and 19, 1902,

Between the INTERNATIONAL ASSOCIATION OF BRIDGE AND STRUC-
TURAL IRONWORKERS, represented by Mr. Frank Buchanan,
President, and Mr. D. F. McIntyre, Secretary and Treasurer,
and the AMERICAN BRIDGE COMPANY OF NEW YORK, represented
by Mr. S. P. Mitchell, Chief Engineer, and Mr. H. F. Lofland,
Erecting Manager, Eastern Division, for the purpose of dis-
cussing a working agreement between the Association and the
Company.

The following paragraphs were passed upon and again submitted to the Company by the International Executive Board after their meeting in Pittsburgh, January 20th to 25th; see minutes of meeting:

1. That there shall be no limitation as to the amount of work a workman shall perform during working hours.

2. That there shall be no restriction as to the use of machinery or tools.

3. That there shall be no restriction as to the use of any manufactured material, except prison-made.

4. That no person shall have the right to interfere with the workmen during working hours.

5. That the Company shall be at liberty to employ or discharge through its foremen, any journeymen members of the Association or apprentices employed under the Agreement, as it may see fit, but no man is to be discriminated against by reason of his connection in any way with a labor organization.

6. The Association shall not discriminate against the Company by permitting its members to work for other employers, who have not signed a scale of wages equal to the scale agreed upon between the Company and the Association.

7. Where one shift is employed, the number of hours fixed upon to constitute a day's work may be worked between the hours of 6 a. m. and 6 p. m. in cases where the Company finds it to its advantage to shift the regular working hours, on account of trains, tides or other conditions affecting the work, over which it has no control, it being understood, however, that the hours worked are to be consecutive with only the usual interval or cessation of work for meal time, commonly known as "dinner hour."

8. For the time worked in excess of the hours fixed upon to constitute a day's work for one shift, time and half time will be paid, except as stated below. On Sundays throughout the year, February 22nd, Decoration Day, Fourth of July, Thanksgiving Day and Christmas Day, or the days that are observed as these holidays, double time will be paid for any

time worked within the 24 hours constituting the calendar day. No work shall be performed on Labor Day except in case of dire necessity, when the property of the Company is in jeopardy, and the service of the men is required to place the same in safe condition. Double time will be paid for any time worked on Labor Day.

Within the territory fixed upon for the cities of New York, Newark, Philadelphia, Chicago and St. Louis, work may stop at noon Saturday during the months of June, July and August, and double time will be paid for any time worked on Saturday during these months after 12 o'clock noon.

9. In case it is desired by the Company, two separate shifts may be employed on the same piece of work, paying each shift only the regular scale of wages agreed upon for the hours fixed as constituting a day's work. In case of working two shifts the hours of work of the day shift may be arranged by the consent of the Company and the men, as may be most advantageous, but the hours of employment of each shift not be less than the hours fixed upon to constitute a day's work. No member of the Association will be allowed to work in two shifts unless he is paid at the over-time rate, for all work performed in excess of the hours fixed upon as a day's work.

10. The Company will pay the men employed on regular pay days, at least twice every month. Where legal enactments require it, and where it is the local custom and practicable, by reason of the work being located near enough to the Division Office, the men will be paid weekly. The custom will be that no more than one week's time will be held back except in cases where the work is located at such a distance from the Division Office as to make this impracticable.

11. The following branches of work are to be covered by the Agreement. The erection and construction of bridges and viaducts, either steel or cast iron, steel stacks, steel coal bunkers, steel grain elevators and tanks, steel stand pipes, steel water tanks, steel towers, blast furnaces, stoves, and all work pertaining thereto, and all steel or cast iron work pertaining

to buildings, including foundation beams, columns, beams or girders, and structural work for safe deposit vaults; also the wrecking of bridges, viaducts, and steel buildings, the erection and removal of all necessary falsework or scaffolding, and any work required to change or alter in the field material shipped from the shops, such as framing, cutting, bending and drilling. In addition to the above classes of work, the Agreement will cover the following work, where the Unions handling same are amalgamated with this Association: Sidewalk vault light frames, stairways, metallic lathing, metal ceilings, rolling steel curtains, ornamental front work (solid or shell) and corrugated sheet work when attached to steel frames. Isolated pieces, such as plates, anchors, caps, corbels, light lintels, etc., may be set by other mechanics. The framing of lumber for false-works and travelers, and the framing and placing of lumber for the wooden floors of any structures may be done by carpenters or other mechanics. Operating machinery in draw bridges, or other structures may be set and adjusted by other mechanics.

12. When Foremen are members of the Association, they shall not be subject to the rules of the Association while acting as Foremen, and no fines or penalties shall be entered against them by the Association while acting in such capacity.

13. Whenever two or more journeymen members of the Association are working together on a piece of work, a steward may be selected from one of their number to represent the Association. The man selected to act as steward shall not leave his work or interfere with workmen during working hours, and shall perform his duties as an employe of the Company.

14. For the purpose of interpreting the Agreement made between the Company and the Association, for the settling of all disputes that may arise between the Company and the Association, and to decide upon and regulate all matters of mutual interest during the life of the said Agreement, Boards of Referees shall be appointed as follows:

In each of the Three Divisions, into which the United States is divided by the Company, and known by it as the Eastern, Pittsburgh and Western Divisions, each party shall appoint one member to serve on a Board of Referees for the regulating of all questions arising under the Agreement, in each of the respective Divisions. The headquarters of these boards shall be New York for the Eastern Division, Pittsburgh for the Pittsburgh Division, and Chicago for the Western Division. Each party will then appoint one additional man who will serve as a member of each of the Three Boards, so that each Board in each Division will consist of four members, two of which will be appointed by the Company and two by the Association. The members of the Board of Referees shall be appointed to serve for one year, dated from the date of the Agreement. The members so appointed may be removed from time to time by the Association or the Company respectively, if it is found that the appointee is unsuitable for membership of the Board. Any vacancy occurring in the Boards shall be filled by the Company or the Association respectively appointing a member to fill said vacancy.

15. All questions that may arise between the Company and the Association under the Agreement, and all matters of mutual interest, shall first be referred to the two local members of the Board in the Division in which the question arises, who shall render a decision within six days after receipt of notice that their services are required. If these two members of the Board cannot agree, the two additional members constituting the Board may be called in, and the matter re-submitted for adjustment, and a decision must be rendered within six days after said additional members have received notice that their services are required. If the four members constituting the Board cannot agree, a fifth person will be selected by the said Board, the said person to be in no wise identified with organized labor or the bridge building industry, nor shall he be an incumbent of any elective political office. The question at issue shall be submitted to the Board of Five so constituted, and a decision shall be rendered within six days, after the fifth member is selected, and signifies his intention of serving on the board. The decision rendered by the Board

of Five so constituted, shall be final and binding on both parties.

16. The Company and the Association will respectively assume the expense in connection with the meetings of the Boards, so far as the salaries and expenses of their own members and witnesses are concerned; and any additional expenses that may be incurred over and above the expenses just specified, shall be shared equally by the Company and the Association.

17. Any member of the Association in good standing, or representative of the Company, except a Foreman, shall be eligible for membership in the Boards, provided he holds no elective public office, either municipal, county, state or national. Any member shall be disqualified to act on the Boards and shall cease to be a member thereof, immediately upon his election to any public office of employment.

18. In evidence of good faith and to guarantee the payment of any fines imposed as described below, each party to the Agreement agrees to furnish to the other party a satisfactory bond, said bond to be binding and kept in force for the full amount during the life of the Agreement. In case either party fails, wilfully refuses or neglects to abide by the decision rendered by the Board of Five Referees, as aforesaid, then and in that case upon the motion of either the Company or the Association, a Board of Three Arbitrators shall be selected as described below, to take evidence in the matter and render a decision as to whether or not the accused party has wilfully refused or neglected to abide by the decision of the Board of Five Referees, and shall determine upon any fines to be paid by the delinquent party to the other party, the decision of the said Board of Three Arbitrators being final and binding. The amount so awarded shall in no single case exceed the amount of the bond. In the selection of the Board of Three Referees, the Company will select one member, the Association one, and the two members so selected shall choose the third member. No person shall be eligible for membership on the Board of Arbitrators who is in any way connected with

organized labor or the bridge building industry, or who holds any elective public office, either municipal, county, state or national.

Any expenses that may have to be incurred on account of the appointment of the Board of Three Arbitrators shall be shared equally between the Company and the Association, except the salaries and expenses of the officers, members, employes, witnesses, etc., of the Company and the Association, which expenses will be assumed by the Company and the Association respectively.

19. No strikes, lockouts, stoppages or interferences with any of the work being conducted under the agreement shall be resorted to, pending a decision of the Board of Referees.

20. The Board of Five Referees shall have the power and their decision shall be binding on both the Company and the Association, to make working rules in conformity with the intent of the Agreement, and to pass on any questions that may arise between the parties under the Agreement, but they shall not have the power to change any of the stipulations of the Agreement or to make rules conflicting therewith.

21. The Agreement is to remain in force for one year from the date thereof.

22. Each party to the Agreement must notify the other party at least four months before its expiration of any change of any character whatsoever, which may be desired for the ensuing year.

23. It is agreed that there is to be no infringement of the noon hour, except by mutual agreement between the foreman on a piece of work and the majority of his men.

24. The Agreement is intended to cover work performed by the Company's forces within the territory included within the United States of America. When the Company contemplates sending structural ironworkers to perform work outside of the United States, it agrees to give preference to members of the Association, and in such cases special agreements will be made with the men sent, as may be found advisable to suit the varying conditions. The Company or firm agrees to

notify the Association when the services of such men are required.

25. The Association agrees to furnish upon the demand of the Company or its representatives, as many of the various classes of experienced structural ironworkers as the Company may require for the protection of its work, in any part of the territory covered by the Agreement; but in the event of a failure or inability on the part of the Association to furnish the men called for, the Company shall be at liberty to employ any other men not members of the Association, as it may see fit, without in any way violating the Agreement or giving cause for strikes, stoppages or interferences with the work. It being understood, however, that men so employed shall not receive less than the prevailing rate of wages agreed upon for the place or district in question. It is further agreed that when the Company calls upon the Association to furnish structural iron workers, that only experienced men or those who have been employed at least eighteen months on erection work will be furnished.

26. In cases where the Company furnishes transportation for men from one point to another or allows them time while traveling, and where any of the men so transported fail to go to work or leave the work for which they have been engaged before earning sufficient money to reimburse the Company for the amounts paid for traveling expenses or time allowed, then and in such cases, the Association agrees to furnish at its own expense, a man or men to take the place of the man or men who have failed to go to work or have left the work as above stated. The Company agrees that when the men have remained on such work until its completion, to furnish them return transportation to the point from which they had been originally taken. It being understood that men will not be engaged and sent to any piece of work under misrepresentation on the part of the Company, as to the conditions existing at the point to which they are sent.

27. As far as the Company is concerned, it will not object to the business agent of the Association visiting the work,

provided said business agent does not talk to, call off or in any way interfere with the men employed during working hours.

28. The Company agrees that after material has been unloaded on the site of the work, the handling of the same is to be done by members of the Association, or the apprentices as herein provided, except when it is necessary to use tackle or derricks, the unloading of material is to be done by members of the Association or apprentices where the tackles or derricks are the property of the Company.

29. A sympathetic strike ordered by other trades, or by one of the central bodies, where it is necessary to take part to protect union principles, shall not be considered a violation of this Agreement.

30. In the erection of buildings and small structures, or in the erection of bridges which are operated from one side of the stream, but one non-union foreman shall be employed, but when the work is so divided as to make it necessary to work it in sections, or when the bridges are sufficiently large to make it advantageous to separate the erection of the false-work and the steel work, or on bridges that are worked in sections as from both sides of a stream, or in the erection of viaducts which are operated from both ends of the structure or in any instance where one section is separated and removed from the other, more than one non-union foreman may be employed; but in no instance shall more than two such non-union foremen be employed on one piece of work.

31. The Company shall have the right to employ apprentices, and such apprentices shall serve on erection work for a period of not less than eighteen months before being eligible for membership in the Association or before receiving the rates of wages agreed upon for members of the Association. No man shall be employed as an apprentice whose age is over thirty-five years.

32. The Association agrees to the employment of apprentices in the ratio of one apprentice to every ten bridgemen or structural iron workers employed, members of the Association.

33. When the Company is the original contractor, and sublets the work to another firm or company, the sub-contractor
shall be subject to all the terms and conditions of this Agreement.

Hours, Rates of Wages and Jurisdiction Asked for by the Association.

Jurisdiction.	Hours.	Rates per Hour. Cents.
Chicago	Cook County	8	50
New York	25 miles	8	50
Pittsburgh	75 miles	8	50
Boston	50 miles	8	40
Washington	25 miles	8	40
Buffalo	100 miles	8	45
Milwaukee	50 miles	8	45
Kansas City	50 miles	8	50
Newark	25 miles	8	50
Albany	25 miles	9	40
Philadelphia	50 miles	8	50
Baltimore	50 miles	8	43¾
Cleveland	100 miles	8	50
St. Louis	150 miles	8	50
Minneapolis	50 miles	8	40
Wheeling	State of W. Va.	8	50
Omaha	50 miles	8	45
Scranton	50 miles	8	40
Denver	State of Colorado	8	45
Detroit	25 miles	8	43¾
Cincinnati	75 miles	8	40
Salt Lake City	50 miles	8	40
San Francisco	50 miles	8	40
Richmond	25 miles	8	45
Portland, Ore.	State of Oregon	8	40
Indianapolis	50 miles	8	40

Outside of the limits fixed for cities described
above 9   40

Principles and Working Rules Relating to the Employment of Bridge and Structural Ironworkers in the Erection of Bridges, Buildings, etc.

Eight hours shall constitute a day's work in localities where it is now the prevailing custom to work eight hours. In other localities nine hours shall constitute a day's work; this, however, may be subject to arbitration.

Time and half-time will be allowed for time worked in excess of the hours fixed upon as constituting a day's work for one shift, except as follows:

On Sundays throughout the year, Decoration Day, Fourth of July, Thanksgiving Day, Christmas Day or the days observed as these holidays, double time will be allowed for any time worked within the twenty-four hours constituting a calendar day. No work shall be performed on Labor Day except in case of dire necessity, when the property of the employer is in jeopardy and the service of the men is required to place the same in a safe condition; double time will be paid for any time worked on Labor Day. Only straight time will be allowed for time worked on Saturday afternoon, but a half-holiday Saturday afternoon without pay may be granted by arrangement between the employer and the workmen.

When two separate shifts are employed on the same piece of work, each shift will be paid the regular prevailing rate of wages per hour. Hours for each shift may be arranged between the employer and workmen as may be most advantageous, but the hours of employment of each shift will not be less than the hours fixed upon as constituting a day's work.

Workmen will be paid every two weeks upon pay days fixed by the employer, except in localities where it is required by law or where it is the prevailing custom to pay weekly.

It will be the general custom to withhold not more than one week's time, to enable the employer to prepare the payrolls, etc.

When any workman is discharged or laid off, he shall be paid in full within twenty-four hours.

When a workman leaves the service of an employer of his own accord he will receive the pay due him at the next regular payday.

There shall be no restriction or discrimination on the part of workmen as to the handling of any materials entering into the construction of the work upon which they are employed.

There shall be no limitation placed upon the amount of work performed by any workman during working hours.

There shall be no restriction as to the use of machinery or tools or as to the number of men employed in the operation of same.

There shall be no restriction whatever as to the employment of foremen.

There shall be no sympathetic strikes called on account of trades disputes.

No persons other than those authorized by the employer shall interfere with workmen during working hours.

The employer may employ or discharge, through his representative, any workman as he may see fit; but no workman is to be discriminated against on account of his connection with a labor organization.

There shall be no discrimination against, interference with, or fines imposed upon foremen who have been in the service of the employer during the time of strike.

Apprentices to learn the trade may be employed in proportion of one apprentice to every seven bridgemen and such apprentices shall serve on erection work for a period of not less than six months before being eligible for membership in a labor organization, or before receiving the wages agreed upon for members of such organization. No man shall be employed as an apprentice whose age is over thirty years. The apprentices shall perform such duties as may be assigned to them by the foreman in charge.

Laborers may be employed for unloading and handling

materials in yards and storage points and for the removal of materials from such yards or storage points to the site of the work.

Such work as the framing of falsework and travelers, the framing and placing of wooden decks (ties and guard rails) and all woodwork on mill buildings, the painting of structural steel and iron work and the placing and adjusting of operating machinery in other structures may be performed by such men as the employer may select.

In cases where misunderstandings or disputes arise between the employer and workmen, the matter in question shall be submitted to arbitration locally, without strikes, lock-outs or the stoppage of work pending the decision of the arbitrators.

Effective from May 1, 1903, to January 1, 1905.

(Clause pertaining to Philadelphia.)

Wages to be 50 cents per hour for first class bridgemen and jurisdiction of Local No. 13 to the territory within a radius of 50 miles from the City Hall of Philadelphia.

Signed

H. F. LOFLAND,
M. J. CUNNANE.

Working Rules

as agreed upon between Local Unions Nos. 11, 35, 40, 45 and 52 of the International Association of Bridge and Structural Iron Workers and the Eastern District Committee of the National Association of Erectors of Structural Steel and Iron Work.

Effective until January 1st, 1906.

District of New York City and Vicinity.

Embracing

the territory within a radius of Thirty-five (35) miles of N. Y. City City Hall and all of Long Island.

This Agreement shall go into effect immediately and shall expire January 1, 1906, and applies only to the territory within a radius of thirty-five (35) miles of the City Hall of New York, and all of Long Island.

Art. 1.—Eight (8) hours shall constitute a day's work.

Art. 2. Bridgemen will be employed at the rate of fifty-six and one-fourth (56¼c) cents per hour and apprentices will receive thirty-one and one-fourth (31¼c) cents per hour.

Art. 3. Time and half time will be allowed for time worked in excess of the hours constituting a day's work for one shift, except as follows:

Art. 4. On Sundays, throughout the year, New Year's Day, Washington's Birthday, Decoration Day, Fourth of July, Labor Day, Thanksgiving Day and Christmas Day, or on the days that may be observed as these holidays, double time will be allowed for any time worked within the twenty-four (24) hours constituting the calendar day. No work shall be performed on Labor Day, except in case of dire necessity, where the property of the employer is in jeopardy, and where the service of the men is required to place same in safe condition. A half-holiday on Saturday afternoons throughout the year, without pay, will be granted. Any work performed on Saturday afternoon will be paid for at double time.

Art. 5. When two (2) separate shifts are employed on the same piece of work, the men in each shift will be paid the regular straight time rate of wages per hour. The hours for each shift may be arranged between the employer and the workmen, as may be most advantageous, but the hours of employment on each shift will not be less than the hours fixed upon as constituting a day's work.

Art. 6. Barring delays from causes beyond the control of the employer, workmen will be paid on the job once a week upon pay days to be fixed by the employer.

Art. 7. It will be the general custom to withhold not more than three (3) days' time to enable the employer to prepare the pay rolls, etc.

Art. 8. When any workman is discharged, or laid off, he shall be paid in full at the office within twenty-four (24) hours, upon presentation by him of time check, provided the work upon which he is engaged is located in Manhattan. If the work is located outside of Manhattan he will be paid on the job.

Art. 9. When a workman leaves the service of an employer of his own accord, he will receive the pay due him on the next regular pay day.

Art. 10. There shall be no restriction or discrimination on the part of a Union or workman as to the handling of any materials entering into the construction of the work upon which they are employed.

Art. 11. There shall be no limitation placed by a Union or workman upon the amount of work to be performed by any workman during working hours.

Art. 12. There shall be no restriction on the part of a Union or workman as to the use of machinery or tools, or to the number of men required to handle or operate same.

Art. 13. There shall be no restriction on the part of a Union or workman whatever as to the employment of foremen. The employer may employ on one piece of work as many foremen as in his judgment are necessary for the safe, expeditious and economical handling of same, regardless of whether such foremen are members of a Union or not.

Art. 14. A Union or workman shall not take part in any sympathetic strike whatsoever, until the question in dispute is arbitrated under Article 23 provided for that purpose.

Art. 15. No persons other than those authorized by the employer shall interfere with workmen during working hours. The Union, however, may appoint a steward on each job. All complaints or grievances shall originate with the job steward and the representative of the employer on the job, and shall be made in duplicate in writing, one copy to be given to the representative of the employer, and one copy to the Union or their representative.

Art. 16. The employer may employ or discharge through his representative any workman as he may see fit, but no workman is to be discriminated against solely on account of his connection with a labor organization.

Art. 17. There shall be no discrimination against, interference with or fines imposed upon foremen who have been in the service of an employer during the time of a strike.

Art. 18. The Union shall, upon demand, furnish the employer with a sufficient number of competent workmen to meet his requirements, and, in case the Union fails to do so, the employer shall be at liberty to employ such other men as may be found by the employer or his representative to be satisfactory as to character and competency.

Art. 19. Workmen classified as "Bridgemen" and entitled to receive the rate of wages agreed upon for bridgemen, will be skilled mechanics and shall be competent to perform such work as the erection of structural steel and iron and ornamental metal work; the rigging and handling of travelers and other important mechanical appliances used in the erection of work; the erecting in place and connecting of members entering permanently into a structure, and the driving of field rivets.

Art. 20. Apprentices may be employed in the proportion

of one (1) apprentice to every seven (7) bridgemen, and such apprentices shall serve on erection work for a period of not less than one and one-half (1½) years before being eligible for membership in a bridge and structural iron workers' union, and before receiving the rate of wages agreed upon for bridgemen. No man shall be employed as an apprentice whose age is over thirty (30) years. Apprentices shall perform such duties as may be assigned to them by the foreman in charge, the intention being that apprentices shall be given such varied duties from time to time as will enable them to learn the trade and fit them for the position of bridgemen.

Art. 21. Laborers may be employed for the unloading and handling of materials in yards, and at storage points, and for the distribution of materials in same. Laborers may also be employed for the handling and delivering of materials from yards and other storage points to the site of the work—site of work being understood to mean:

(a) In the case of buildings, within reach of the derricks or other appliances used in erecting the materials.

(b) In the case of bridges, viaducts and similar structures, to the point of the structure nearest the storage yard.

In the case of removing old structures, laborers may be employed for the removing of the materials after same have been dismantled and landed by the bridgemen.

Art. 22. Such work as the framing of falsework, the framing of travelers, the framing and placing of wooden decks (including ties and guard rails) and all wood work on mill buildings, the placing and adjusting of operating machinery in drawbridges and machinery in other structures and the field painting of structures may be performed by such men as the employer may select irrespective of their connection with any Union.

Art. 23. In case of misunderstandings or disputes arising between an employer and his workmen, the matter in question shall be submitted to arbitration locally without strikes, lockouts or stoppage of work, pending the decision of the arbitrators. These arbitrators shall consist of two (2) representatives appointed by the employer and two (2) representatives appointed by the Union, and these four (4) so appointed shall select a fifth (5th), who shall be a disinterested party, and the decision of the arbitrators shall be rendered within six (6) days and be final and binding upon both parties, and not subject to appeal. None of the definite articles of these rules shall be subject to arbitration.

MEMORANDUM

OF

AGREEMENT

LOCAL No. 40

UNITED HOUSESMITHS' AND BRIDGEMEN'S UNION

OF NEW YORK.

MEMORANDUM OF AGREEMENT, Entered into this 23d day of January, 1905, by and between the IRON LEAGUE ERECTORS' ASSOCIATION, EMPLOYERS' ASSOCIATION OF ARCHITECTURAL IRON WORKERS, ORNAMENTAL BRONZE AND IRON MASTERS, all of the City of New York, Associations by their officers duly authorized, parties of the first part, and the District Council of the UNITED HOUSESMITHS' AND BRIDGEMEN'S UNION, OF NEW YORK AND VICINITY, comprising the following locals of the International Association of Bridge and Structural Iron Workers:

Local No. 35, United Housesmiths' and Bridgemen's Union of Brooklyn.

Local No. 45, Bridge and Structural Iron Workers of New Jersey.

Local No. 52, United Housesmiths' and Bronze Erectors of New York.

Local No. 40, United Housesmiths' and Bridgemen's Union of New York.

Local No. 11, United Housesmiths' and Bridgemen's Union

of Newark, N. J., by their officers duly authorized, parties of
the second part.

WITNESSETH :

First—This agreement shall apply only to men employed
in the erection of structural steel and ornamental iron and
bronze work, within a radius of thirty-five (35) miles from
the New York City Hall, in the States of New York and New
Jersey and including the whole of Long Island. It shall take
effect immediately and continue in force until January 1st,
1906, and thereafter from year to year unless either party
hereto shall have given three (3) months notice in writing to
the party of the other part, prior to the expiration of any
year, of a desire to change the agreement for the following
year.

Second—The parties of the first part agree to employ only
members of the UNITED HOUSESMITHS AND BRIDGEMEN OF NEW
YORK AND VICINITY. It is agreed, however, in case the Union
is unable to supply competent workmen in sufficient quantity,
the parties of the first part shall be at liberty to hire other
men who may apply, and who have been examined and found
satisfactory as to character and competency, by the parties
of the first part or their representatives. The parties of the
second part shall be at liberty to admit such men to membership in their Union, and the parties of the first part shall not
in any way prevent or oppose the said employees from joining said Union.

Third—All men to be employed and paid by the hour.
Eight (8) hours to constitute a day's work, except on Saturdays, when work shall cease at twelve o'clock. Overtime shall
be paid for at the rate of time and one-half except on Saturday afternoons, Sundays, and the following legal holidays,
viz: Washington's Birthday, Decoration Day, Fourth of July,
Labor Day, Thanksgiving Day, Christmas Day, and New
Year's Day, or on the days that may be observed as these
holidays, for which double time will be paid. Unless abso-
lutely required no work is done on Sundays or legal holidays.
No work is to be done on Labor Day, and no man is to be dis-

charged for refusing to work overtime except in the case of accident or actual necessity. The parties of the second part agree to work in regular night gangs, at regular time, wages and hours.

Fourth—The parties of the first part agree to pay weekly on the job at regular pay days.

Fifth—No apprentice to be employed by the parties of the first part without the written consent of his parents or guardian to such employment, and shall serve a term of one and one-half (1½) years in case of structural apprentices. At the end of such time, said apprentice may become a member of the Union, provided he passes the necessary examination. The ratio of apprentices on structural work to be not more than one (1) apprentice to every seven (7) skilled mechanics.

Sixth—The Union to appoint a Steward on each job. All complaints shall originate either with the job steward, or the representative of the employer on the job, and shall be made in duplicate in writing, one copy to be given to the business agent or representative of the parties of the first part, and one copy to the parties of the second part or their representatives.

Seventh—All grievances or complaints which cannot be satisfactorily adjusted between the individual employer and the parties of the second part or their representatives, shall be submitted to the joint Board of Conciliation of the Iron trade, which shall consist of three (3) employers elected by the industry, and an equal number of representatives of the parties of the second part, who shall be elected by the UNITED HOUSESMITHS AND BRIDGEMEN OF NEW YORK AND VICINITY, from among members of said Union, who are at the time of their service on said board regularly in the employ of some employers, members of the parties of the first part, or BUILDING TRADE EMPLOYERS' ASSOCIATION. A majority vote of the said Board shall be conclusive in relation to all matters submitted to it and in case of a tie vote, the said Board shall have power to agree upon an Umpire or Referee, whose vote shall be similarly conclusive and binding, and the parties hereto agree to abide by the decision of the Board. The BOARD OF CONCILIA-

TION will form such rules as may be necessary to govern its own proceedings.

Eighth—In consideration of the mutual covenants herein contained, the parties of the second part hereby agree not to take part in any sympathetic strike whatsoever, and they hereby agree not to go out on strike until after any grievances have been submitted to the BOARD OF CONCILIATION above referred to and a decision reached. The parties of the first part hereto agree not to order or carry out any lock-outs until in like manner any grievance has been submitted to the BOARD OF CONCILIATION above referred to and a decision reached.

Ninth—The parties of the first part hereby agree to pay the following wages:

All men employed on structural work except apprentice work at the rate of 56¼ cents per hour.

Finishers, 56¼ cents per hour.

Finishers Helpers, 37½ cents per hour.

Apprentices, 31¼ cents per hour.

Finishers helpers not to be employed on structural work. In finishing work, it is understood that one helper to be allowed to one finisher, in the erection of work.

Tenth—The parties of the first part shall be at liberty to employ such men as they see fit in unloading trucks, in framing false work, in painting and handling material for storage purposes at storage points. It is understood that when material is delivered at the building within reach of the derricks, that the handling of same shall be done afterwards by members of the Union.

Eleventh—There shall be no restriction or discrimination on the part of the workmen as to the handling of any materials entering into the construction work upon which they are employed.

Twelfth—There shall be no restriction placed by any workman or the Union upon the amount of work to be performed by any workman during working hours. There shall be no restriction on the part of any workman or the Union as to the use of machinery or tools, or as to the number of men required to handle or operate same.

Thirteenth—There shall be no restriction whatever as to the employment of foremen. The employer may employ on one piece of work as many foremen as in his judgment are necessary for the safe, expeditious and economical handling of same, and it is understood that the foremen so employed are not to become members of any Union and that no foreman shall be discriminated against by the Union.

Fourteenth—No person, or persons, other than those herein expressly authorized shall have the right to interfere with workmen during working hours.

Fifteenth—In the erection of bronze work, in the employment of men, preference will be given to the parties of the second part, provided the same are competent.

Sixteenth—The parties of the first part shall have the right to employ any foreman on their work as a pusher or skilled mechanic without his being obliged to have the card of the Union; this is only to apply as a temporary measure and as soon as practicable and possible the foreman is to return to his regular duties. Not more than two (2) such men to be employed on any job at one time and for not more than two (2) weeks and for not longer than eight (8) weeks in all during the year. No foreman can work under this clause for any employer unless he has worked in the capacity for such employer immediately before.

Seventeenth—The Joint Arbitration Plan adopted in conference, July 3d and 9th, 1903, between the Unions of New York City and the Building Trades Employers' Association, shall be a part of this agreement, and both parties shall be governed according to its provisions.

IN WITNESS WHEREOF, the parties have hereto this day, set

171

their hands and seals, the day and year first herein above mentioned.

Signed

IRON LEAGUE ERECTORS' ASSOCIATION,
By John Cooper, President.
EMPLOYERS' ASSOCIATION ARCHITECTURAL
IRON WORKERS,
By Robert T. McMurray, President.
BRONZE IRON MASTERS,
By A. S. Richey, President.
DISTRICT COUNCIL UNITED HOUSESMITHS AND
BRIDGEMEN OF NEW YORK AND VICINITY,
By Charles Massey, President,
William Green, Secretary.

WORKING AGREEMENT

OF THE

UNITED HOUSESMITH AND BRIDGEMEN INTERNATIONAL UNION,
LOCAL NO. 13, OF PHILADELPHIA, PA.

Article I.

The party of the first part agrees to employ only members who are in good standing in Local 13, or who have declared their intentions of becoming members of Local 13. In the event of the party of the second part being unable to supply the required number of men to the party of the first part, they shall be at liberty to employ such men as may qualify as mechanics, and who are willing to become members of Local 13.

Article II.

The party of the first part shall be at liberty to employ such men as they believe qualified for unloading material at storage points, and at storage points only. The sorting or distributing of all material at any point in or about the job shall be performed by members of Local No. 13.

Article III.

The party of the second part agrees to work in regular shifts, at regular hours, time and wages, when two or three shifts are required, but when a man is requested to work in more than one shift he shall be paid at the rate of double time for all work performed over eight hours. When a member is requested to start work before 8 a. m. he shall be paid at the rate of double time. All work performed by the party of the second part above eight hours shall be paid for at the rate of double time. When only one shift is required, the eight hours shall be made between 8 a. m. and 5 p. m. By mutual consent of both parties, the noon hour may be curtailed.

Article IV.

Eight hours shall constitute a day's work, except on Saturday, when all work shall cease at noon.

Article V.

The party of the first part agrees to pay weekly on the job on regular stated pay days. Waiting time shall be paid at the rate of double time, when the men are compelled to wait for wages due them after the regular stated pay day.

Article VI.

It shall be the general custom not to hold more than three days' pay to enable the employer to prepare the pay roll.

Article VII.

It is understood that the men's wages due them on the regular pay day must be paid them not later than one hour after the men stop work on the regular stated pay day; otherwise double time shall be paid the men after that time.

Article VIII.

Holidays, or days observed as such, New Year's Day, Washington's Birthday, Decoration Day, Fourth of July, Thanksgiving Day, Christmas Day, and from Saturday noon until Sunday midnight, the scale of wages for work done on these days shall be paid for at the rate of double time. No work shall be performed by any member of Local 13 on Labor Day.

Article IX.

No member shall be discriminated against for refusing to work on holidays or overtime, or because he retains membership in Local 13.

Article X.

Men who are discharged or laid off shall be paid off within twenty-four hours, on the job, or at the office if in the City of Philadelphia; if outside of the City of Philadelphia, the members who are discharged or laid off shall be paid off on the job, or transportation furnished him to the office of the company he was employed by.

Article XI.

Apprentices shall be allowed at the ratio of one apprentice to every seven mechanics, and his duties shall be of such work as will enable him to become a skilled mechanic, but under no consideration will he be allowed to have charge of any part of the work while serving his apprenticeship, such as handling plans or issuing orders, and it is understood that no apprentice shall be employed by any contractor who has not got the required number of mechanics in his employ. No apprentice to be over twenty-five years of age, and he shall serve an apprenticeship of eighteen months before he is eligible for membership as a mechanic in Local 13.

Article XII.

The business representative shall appoint a steward on each job, who shall perform his duties as steward at such times as will not interfere with his regular work, and should any grievance arise on the job with his own trade or any trade affiliated with the Building Trades Department, he shall notify the business agent of his organization. The business agent shall use every means to adjust all grievances without the stopping of work. A strike called by the Building Trades Department, or by the Central Labor Union, or by the International Association of Bridge and Structural Iron Workers, to support trade union rules, shall in no way be termed a violation of this agreement.

Article XIII.

Timekeepers shall not perform nor do any work in or about any job unless they carry a card in Local 13.

Article XIV.

There shall be but one foreman allowed on any job. Assistant foreman and all others shall be members of Local 13.

Article XV.

The business representative of Local 13 shall be allowed to visit all jobs at all times.

Article XVI.

Riveting gangs shall be composed of not less than four men at all times.

Article XVII.

Local 13 will be responsible for members that ship out of town on jobs in the jurisdiction of this agreement, it being understood that the men must ship out through the office of this Union, and transportation to be paid by the employer.

Article XVIII.

When contractors ship men out of town through the representative of Local 13, it is understood that traveling time shall be paid the men at the rate of sixty (60) cents per hour. This to apply to the amount of time they are traveling.

Article XIX.

When contractors send men from one job to another, they shall pay the car fare for the men, and the men shall also be paid for the time of going from one job to the other. It is understood that the men shall go by the most direct car line when sent from one job to the other, or they will not be paid by their employers for the time of traveling.

It is further understood that when men are requested to report on any job, and the work is not ready, and the contractor, or his representative, requests the men to wait on the job, they shall be paid for the time they are waiting.

Article XX.

Contractors who take men out of town on work which is in the jurisdiction of this agreement, and when the men are compelled to remain idle for six days, their board shall be paid by the employer; otherwise the employer shall ship the men back to their local.

Article XXI.

Finishers' helpers shall be employed at the ratio of one helper to each finisher.

Article XXII.

This Union forbids piece work of all kinds.

Article XXIII.

There shall be no laborers employed on the job, except to carry bolts, rivets or coal; all other work is to be done by members of Local 13.

Article XXIV.

The scale of wages shall be as follows: Men classed as bridgemen, sixty (60) cents per hour, $4.80 per day. For eight-hour men, classed as finishers, sixty (60) cents per hour, or $4.80 per day for eight hours. Men classed as finishers' helpers, forty-five (45) cents per hour, or $3.60 for eight hours.

Apprentices shall be paid according to their ability.

Article XXV.

Territory covered by this agreement shall be the County of Philadelphia and two hundred (200) miles from the County of Philadelphia where no organization holds jurisdiction over, as was granted them by the International Association of Bridge and Structural Iron Workers of America.

Article XXVI.

This agreement to go into effect on May 1, 1912, and to continue until April 30, 1913, and from there on from year to year, unless by mutual consent, and on three months' notice by either party shall this agreement be discontinued after April 30, 1913.

Signed for Local 13 by

By ....

Signed for Contractor

By ....

No signed agreements.   *Pittsburgh.*

Working Rules Relating to the Employment of Members of Local Union No. 3, of the International Association of Bridge, Structural and Ornamental Iron Workers.

Article I.

Eight hours shall constitute a day's work in the Pittsburgh district. Time and one-half time will be allowed for time worked in excess of the hours fixed upon as constituting a day's work for one shift, except as follows:

Article II.

On Sunday through the year, Decoration Day, Fourth of July, Thanksgiving Day, and Christmas Day, or the days observed as those holidays, and after 12 o'clock noon Saturday throughout the year double time shall be allowed. No work shall be performed on Labor Day, except in case of dire necessity, where the property of the employer is in jeopardy, and where the services of the men is required to place the same in safe condition. Double time will be allowed for any time worked on Labor Day.

Article III.

When two or more shifts are employed on the same work, the men in each shift shall be paid the regular straight time rate of wages per hour. The hours for each shift may be arranged between the employer and workmen, as may be most advantageous, but the hours of employment on each shift will not be less than the hours fixed upon as constituting a day's work. When one shift is employed, the hours of work shall be between 8 a. m. and 5 p. m., except in cases of necessity, or when otherwise mutually agreed upon between the employer and employes.

Article IV.

Workmen will be paid every week at 12 o'clock noon Saturday on job. It will be the general custom to withhold not more than one and a half (1½) days' time to enable the employer to prepare the pay roll.

Article V.

When any workman is discharged or laid off, he shall be paid in full within twenty-four hours on the job. When a workman leaves the service of an employer of his own accord, he will receive the pay due him on the next regular pay day.

Article VI.

There shall be no limitation placed upon the amount of work to be performed by any workman during working hours. There shall be no restriction on the part of the Union or workmen as to the use of machinery or tools, or the number of men required to handle or operate the same.

Article VII.

There shall be no restriction on the part of the Union or workmen as to the employment of foremen. The employer may employ on one piece of work as many foremen as in his judgment are necessary for the safe, expeditious and economical handling of the same, regardless of whether such foremen are members of the Union or not, so long as such foremen do not perform the work of journeymen, or act in the capacity of "Pusher," except where a foreman is employed temporarily, for the sole purpose of retaining him in the service of the employer.

Article VIII.

No person other than those authorized by the employer shall interfere with workmen during working hours, and in no case shall stewards, when employed on the work, transact any business in connection with his Union, or interfere with other workmen during working hours.

Article IX.

This Union, upon demand, is to furnish the employer with a sufficient number of competent workmen to meet his requirements, and in case the Union fails to do so, the employer shall be at liberty to employ other men. In this case mutually satisfactory arrangements, as to the transportation, are to be made with Secretary of the Local Union in advance.

Article X.

Workmen classified as Bridgemen, and entitled to receive the rate of wages as agreed upon for Bridgemen, shall be skilled mechanics, and shall be competent to perform such work as the erection, rigging and handling of travelers and other important appliances used in the erection of work, the erecting in place and connecting of members entering permanently into a structure, and driving of field rivets under competent foremen.

Article XI.

Apprentices may be employed in the proportion of one Apprentice to every seven (7) Bridgemen, and such Apprentice shall serve on erection work for a period of not less than one year and a half before being eligible for membership in a Bridge and Structural Iron Workers' Union, and before receiving the rate of wages agreed upon for Bridgemen. No man shall be employed as an Apprentice who is over thirty-five years of age. Apprentices shall perform such duties as may be assigned to them by the foreman in charge; the intention being that the Apprentices shall be given such varied duties from time to time as will enable him to learn the trade and fit him for the position of a Bridgeman. Apprentices shall receive not less than 40 cents an hour.

Article XII.

Laborers may be employed for the unloading and handling of materials in yards and storage points, so long as such material is handled by hand, and no rigging or machinery is used to handle same.

Article XIII.

In case of removal of old structures, members of the Union shall be employed to land, dismember and remove same, except such material as can be removed by hand, and no rigging or machinery is used in removing same.

Article XIV.

Such work as the framing, placing and removing of false-work, pile-driving, and the framing and erection of derricks and travelers, and the assembling and erection of all iron and steel in reinforced concrete work in the field, shall be performed by members of the Union.

Article XV.

Framing and placing of wooden decks, including ties and guard rails; the placing and adjusting of operating machinery in draw bridges, and the machinery in other structures, shall be performed by such men as employer may select.

Article XVI.

In case of misunderstandings or disputes arising between an employer and his workmen, the matter in question shall be submitted to arbitration, locally, without strikes, lockouts or stoppage of work, pending a decision of the arbitrators, consisting of three disinterested persons, one to be appointed by the employers, one by the Union, and the third by the two first selected, whose decision shall be rendered within six (6) days, and be final and binding on both parties, and not subject to appeal.

None of the definite articles of these rules shall be subject to arbitration.

Article XVII.

This Agreement shall be effective from May 1, 1914.

Article XVIII.

The jurisdiction of Local Union No. 3 shall not exceed one hundred and thirty-five (135) miles in radius from City Hall, Pittsburgh, Pennsylvania.

Article XIX.

The wages of Bridgemen shall be 62½ cents per hour.

AGREEMENT

BETWEEN THE

ARCHITECTURAL IRON LEAGUE

AND THE

INTERNATIONAL ASSOCIATION BRIDGE AND STRUCTURAL IRON WORKERS' UNION NO. 1 OF CHICAGO.

MAY 1, 1912, TO APRIL 30, 1915.

AGREEMENT.

This agreement, made this 30th day of April, 1912, by and between the Architectural Iron League *et al.* (Employers), party of the first part, and the Bridge and Structural Iron Workers' Union No. 1 of Chicago, of the International Association Bridge and Structural Iron Workers, party of the second part, for the purpose of preventing strikes and lockouts and facilitating a peaceful adjustment of all grievances and disputes which may, from time to time, arise between the employer and mechanics in the Bridge and Structural Iron and Steel trade.

The territory covered by this agreement is a radius of fifty miles from Chicago City Hall.

2. NO OUTSIDE INTERFERENCE.

Witnesseth, that both parties to this agreement hereby covenant and agree that they will not tolerate nor recognize any right of any other association, union, council or body of men, not directly parties hereto, international, national or local, to interfere in any way with the carrying out of this agreement; and that they will use all lawful means to compel their members to comply with the arbitration agreement and working rules as jointly agreed upon and adopted.

3. Principles Upon Which This Agreement Is Based.

Both parties hereto this day hereby adopt the following principles as an absolute basis for their joint working rules, and to govern the action of the Joint Arbitration Board as hereinafter provided for:

1. That there shall be no limitation as to the amount of work a man shall perform during his working day.

2. That there shall be no restriction of the use of machinery or tools.

3. That there shall be no restriction of the use of any manufactured material except prison-made.

4. That no person shall have the right to interfere with workmen during working hours.

5. That the use of apprentices shall not be prohibited.

6. That the foreman shall be the agent of the employer.

7. That all workmen are at liberty to work for whomsoever they see fit.

8. That all employers are at liberty to employ and discharge whomsoever they see fit.

4. Hours.

Eight hours shall constitute a day's work, except on Saturdays during the months of April, May, June, July, August, September, October and November, when work may stop at 12 o'clock noon, with four hours' pay for the day.

5. Overtime.

Time and one-half shall be paid for overtime between the hours of 7 and 8 a. m. and between the hours of 4:30 or 5 and

7 p. m., and for Saturday afternoons during the months of April, May, June, July, August, September, October and November. Where only one shift of men are employed on the job, if the same men work after 7 o'clock p. m. double time shall be paid. Where a single shift is employed, beginning work after 5 p. m., time and one-half shall be paid for the first eight hours and double time thereafter.

6. HOLIDAYS.

Double time to be paid for work done on Sundays throughout the year and also for work done on the following five holidays (or days celebrated as such): Decoration Day, Fourth of July, Thanksgiving Day, Christmas Day and New Year's Day. Sunday and holiday time to cover any time during the twenty-four hours of said calendar days.

7. EXTRA SHIFTS.

Where work is carried on with two or three shifts of men, working eight hours each, then only single time shall be paid for both night and day work during week days, and double time for Sundays and the above mentioned holidays. Where two or three shifts are employed double time shall be paid for all overtime. The regular workday shall be between the hours of 8 a. m. and 5 p. m. Where more than one shift is employed the second shift shall commence work not later than 5 p. m. Where three shifts are employed seven and one-half hours shall constitute a day's work for all shifts, for which a full regular day's pay shall be paid.

8. LABOR DAY.

No work shall be done on Labor Day.

9. WAGES.

The minimum rate of wages to be paid shall be sixty-eight (.68) cents per hour from April 30, 1912, up to and including April 30, 1915, payable in lawful money of the United States or checks. All workmen in this trade shall demand and receive the wages called for in this agreement.

10. Pay Day.

It is agreed that journeymen shall be paid at least every two weeks if paid in currency, or once every week if paid in checks, as agreed between the employer and the employes on the job.

Payment shall be made on the job not later than 5 p. m. every other Tuesday when paid in currency, or, if payment in check is desired, the foreman must be notified not later than Saturday noon preceding.

11. Time and Method of Payment of Wages.

All wages are to be paid on the work in full up to and including the Saturday night preceding pay day. Where a workman quits work of his own accord, he shall receive his pay on the next regular pay day. When a man is discharged, he shall be either paid in cash on the work, or given a time check immediately, which shall be paid at once on presentation at the office of the employer, and if he is not paid promptly upon his arrival at the office, and if he shall remain there during working hours, he shall be paid the minimum wages for such waiting time, Sundays and holidays excepted.

12. Branches of Work Covered by This Agreement.

The following branches of work are covered by this agreement: The erection and construction of bridges, structural steel and cast iron, including steel foundation beams other than rails in buildings, viaducts, steel stacks, coal bunkers, bins or hoppers, whether used for coal, grain, ore, stone or any other material. Hanging ceilings, where dimensions of angles, tees, etc., exceed one and one-half inches. Structural iron and steel work for support of boilers, hoppers, elevators, bank or deposit vaults, derricks, cranes and gas holders, and the jacking up of all elevated roads and bridges, wrecking of bridges, viaducts and structural steel and iron work of fireproof buildings and the erection and removal of all false work from bridges and viaducts, all cast iron or steel mullions except those in store fronts; all frames for openings except those where iron or calomine doors are to be hung; all porches or verandas and balconies except stairs, railings and wire mesh work; all skylights or pent houses except shell ornamental cast work or operating devices; also structural work to support escalators; all cell jail work except doors, stair work, balconies, brackets, wire mesh and bar work; all canopies except where ornamental shell work is attached or intended to be attached; all ventilators, elevator pockets, all exterior wheel or corner guards, overhead travelers made of eye beams or channels; structural work for conveyors for coal, ashes or any other material; all structural steel and iron work for sidewalks and the framing of travelers and derricks. All bulkhead or sluice gate work in connection with pumping stations or dams and locks, also all necessary changes pertaining to this classification of work, such as drilling, chipping, bending, etc.

The setting of isolated pieces, such as plates, caps, corbels, lintels, etc., may be done by other mechanics.

It is further agreed that after the material has been unloaded at the site it shall be handled by members of the party of the second part. When material is unloaded by tackles or derricks, it shall be done by members of the party of the second part.

There shall be no infringement on the noon hour.

Piece work shall not be permitted.

If the party of the first part sublets any portion of his work covered by this agreement, the sub-contractor shall be subject to the terms of this agreement.

13.

No member or members affiliated with the second party shall leave the work of the party of the first part because non-union men in some other line of work or trade are employed on building or job where said second party is employed.

14. FOREMAN.

The foreman—if a union man—shall not be subject to the rules of this union while acting as foreman, and no fines shall be entered against him by his union for any cause whatever, while acting in such capacity; it being understood that a foreman shall be a competent mechanic in his trade and be subject to the decisions of the Joint Arbitration Board. There shall be but one foreman on each job.

15. Steward.

Whenever two or more journeymen members of the second party are working together, a steward may be selected by them from their number to represent them, who shall, while acting as steward, be subject only to the rules and decisions of the Joint Arbitration Board. No salary shall be paid to a journeyman for acting as steward. He shall not leave his work or interfere with workmen during working hours and shall perform his duties as steward so as not to interfere with his duty to his employer. He shall always, while at work, carry a copy of the working rules with him.

16. Apprentices.

Each employer shall have the right to teach his trade to apprentices, and the said apprentices shall serve for a period of not less than ...... years, as prescribed in the apprentice rules to be agreed upon by the Joint Arbitration Board, and shall be subject to control of said Joint Arbitration Board.

17. Arbitration.

Both parties hereto agree that any and all disputes between any member or members of the Employers' Association on the one side, and any member or members of the Union, on the other side, during the life of this agreement, shall be settled by arbitration in the manner herein provided for, and for that purpose both parties hereto agree that they will, at their annual election of each year, elect an Arbitration Committee to serve one year and until their successors are elected and qualified. In case of death, expulsion, removal or disqualification of a member or members on the Arbitration Committee, such vacancy shall be filled by the Association or Union at its next

regular meeting. The Arbitration Committee for each of the
two parties hereto shall consist of five members, and they shall
meet not later than the fourth Tuesday of January of each
year, in joint session, when they shall organize a Joint Arbitration Board by electing a president, vice-president, secretary, treasurer and umpire. The Joint Arbitration Board
shall have full power to enforce this agreement entered into
between the parties hereto, and to make and enforce all lawful
working rules governing both parties. No strikes, lockouts or
stoppage of work shall be resorted to pending the decision of
the Joint Board. When a dispute or grievance arises between
a journeyman and employer (parties hereto), or an apprentice
and his employer, the question at issue shall be submitted in
writing to the presidents of the two organizations, and upon
their failure to agree and settle it, or if one party to the dispute is dissatisfied with the decision, it shall then be submitted
to the Joint Arbitration Board at their next regular meeting.
If the Joint Arbitration Board is unable to agree the umpire
shall be requested to sit with them, and, after he has heard
the evidence, cast the deciding vote. All verdicts shall be decided by majority vote by secret ballot, be rendered in writing
and be final and binding on all the parties to the dispute.

18. Who Are Disqualified to Serve on Arbitration Committee.

No member who is not actively engaged in the trade, or
foreman, nor holds a public office, either elective or appointive,
under the municipal, county, state or national government,
shall be eligible to act as the representative in this trade arbitration board, and any member shall become disqualified to
act as member of this trade Joint Arbitration Board and cease
to be a member thereof immediately upon his election or appointment to any other public office or employment.

19. Umpire.

An umpire shall be selected who is in no wise affiliated or
identified with the building industry, who is not an employe

nor an employer of labor, nor an incumbent of a political elective office.

20. MEETINGS.

The Joint Arbitration Board shall meet to transact routine business the first Tuesday in each month, but special meetings may be called on three days' notice by the president upon application of three members.

The Joint Arbitration Board has the right to summon any member or members affiliated with either party hereto against whom complaints are lodged for breaking this agreement or working rules. and also appear as witness. The summons shall be handed to the president of the association or union to which the member belongs, and he shall cause the member or members to be notified to appear before the Joint Arbitration Board on date set.

21. FINES FOR NON-ATTENDANCE.

Failure to appear when notified, except (in the opinion of the Board) valid excuse is given, shall subject a member to a fine of twenty-five dollars for the first offense, fifty for the second and suspension for the third.

22. SALARIES.

The salary of each representative of the Joint Arbitration Board shall be paid by the Association or Union he represents.

23. QUORUM.

Seven members present shall constitute a quorum in the Joint Arbitration Board, but the chairman of each of the two Arbitration Committees shall have the right to cast the vote in the Joint Arbitration Board for any absent member of his committee.

24. STOPPAGE OF WORK AND PENALTIES

No work under construction by any member or party to this agreement shall be stopped for any cause whatsoever, excepting by joint order signed by the presidents of both organizations, parties to this agreement, or the Joint Arbitration Board, and any member or members affiliated with either of the two parties hereto, violating any part of this agreement or working rules established by the Joint Arbitration Board, shall be subject to a fine of from ten to two hundred dollars, which fine shall be collected by the president of the Association or Union to which the offending member or members belong, and by him paid to the treasurer of the Joint Arbitration Board not later than thirty days after the date of the levying of the fine.

If the fine is not paid by the offender or offenders, it shall be paid out of the treasury of the Association or Union of which the offender or offenders were members at the time the fine was levied against him or them, and within sixty days of date of levying same; or in lieu thereof the Association or Union to which he or they belonged shall suspend the offender or offenders and officially certify such suspension to the Joint Arbitration Board within sixty days from the time of fining, and the Joint Arbitration Board shall cause the suspension decree to be read by the presidents of both the Association and Union at their next regular meeting and then post said decree for sixty days in the meeting rooms of the Association and Union. No one who has been suspended from membership in the Association or Union for neglect or refusal to abide by the decisions of the Joint Arbitration Board can be again admitted to membership except by paying his fine or by unanimous consent of the Joint Arbitration Board.

All fines assessed by the Joint Arbitration Board and collected during the year shall be equally divided between the two parties hereto by the Joint Arbitration Board at the last regular meeting in December.

25. RULES FOR ARBITRATION BOARD AND FOR PARTIES HERETO.

All disputes arbitrated under this agreement must be settled by the Joint Arbitration Board, in conformity with the principles and agreements herein contained, and nothing herein can

be changed by the Joint Arbitration Board. No by-laws or
rules conflicting with this agreement, or working rules agreed
upon, shall be passed or enforced by either party hereto
against any of its affiliated members in good standing.

26. TERMINATION.

It is agreed by the parties hereto that this agreement shall
be in force between the parties hereto from April 30, 1912,
to and including April 30, 1915.

27.

Any individual, firm or corporation signing this agreement
and agreeing to abide thereby, and not affiliated with any
organization connected with the Building Construction Employers' Association, may, with the consent of a majority of
the Arbitration Board and upon payment of an initiation fee
of $50 and $25 per annum to the treasurer of the Joint Arbitration Board, receive the benefits of arbitration herein contained.

These funds to pay expenses of the Joint Arbitration Board,
and, if any balance is left at the annual meeting, same to be
divided equally between the Bridge and Structural Iron Workers' Union No. 1 and the Architectural Iron League *et al.*

All parties to this agreement desiring to send members of
the second party outside of fifty miles radius, a minimum wage
of four dollars and fifty cents ($4.50) for a nine hours' day
shall be paid.

On behalf of the party of the first part:

EDWARD HAUPT,
ADDISON E. WELLS,
ALBERT E. DENNIS,
GEORGE W. GEARY,
JOHN GRIFFITHS.

On behalf of the party of the second part:

JOHN L. WARD,
GEORGE M. CLARK,
JAMES H. MARTIN,
JAMES COUGHLIN,
JOSEPH CARMODY.

Constitution and By-Laws

of

National Erectors' Association.

Constitution.

Article I.—Name.

The name of this Association shall be National Erectors' Association.

Article II.—Membership.

Section 1. Any individual, firm or corporation engaged wholly or in part in the erection of iron and steel bridges, buildings or other structural iron and steel work, shall be eligible to membership upon agreeing to support the principles embodied in the Constitution of this Association.

Sec. 2. The individual, firm or corporation desiring membership shall make application in the form prescribed by the Executive Committee.

A three-fourths' ($\frac{3}{4}$) vote of the General Executive Committee in favor of an applicant shall elect.

Sec. 3. Membership may be terminated upon payment of all dues and assessments to date of termination, as follows:

(a) By resignation after three (3) months' written notice to the General Executive Committee.

(b) By permanent discontinuance of the member's business.

(c) By a three-fourths' ($\frac{3}{4}$) vote of the General Executive Committee.

Article III.—Object.

The object of this Association shall be the institution and maintenance of the Open Shop principle in the employment of labor in the erection of steel and iron bridges and buildings and other structural steel and iron work.

Article IV.—Government.

The government of this Association shall be vested in a General Executive Committee and in District Executive Committees.

The General Executive Committee shall consist of at least five (5) members, and not more than nine (9) members, to be elected annually by the members, each member of the Association being entitled to one (1) vote for every one hundred dollars ($100.00), or majority fraction of one hundred dollars ($100.00), dues paid annually; provided, that every member shall have at least one (1) vote; and provided, that not more than one (1) individual from a single firm shall have membership on the Committee.

The General Executive Committee shall from time to time appoint and fix the salaries and terms of employment of a Commissioner, as the general executive officer, and of such other employes as it may consider necessary.

Article V.—Dues and Assessments.

The expenses of the Association shall be met by monthly dues (and special assessments, when necessary), the amounts of which shall be fixed by the General Executive Committee proportionately to the average number of workmen employed in erection work by each member.

Article VI.—Meetings.

The General Executive Committee and the District Executive Committees shall call all meetings of the whole association membership and of the district membership respectively, and shall fix the time, manner and place for holding same.

Article VII.—Amendments.

This Constitution, except Article III, may be amended at any time by a three-fourths' (¾) vote of the entire membership of the Association, provided that written notice, including a copy of the proposed amendment, shall be given each member at least thirty (30) days in advance of the date of voting thereon.

American Labor: From Conspiracy to Collective Bargaining

AN ARNO PRESS/NEW YORK TIMES COLLECTION

SERIES I

Abbott, Edith.
Women in Industry. 1913.

Aveling, Edward B. and Eleanor M. Aveling.
Working Class Movement in America. 1891.

Beard, Mary.
The American Labor Movement. 1939.

Blankenhorn, Heber.
The Strike for Union. 1924.

Blum, Solomon.
Labor Economics. 1925.

Brandeis, Louis D. and Josephine Goldmark.
Women in Industry. 1907. New introduction by Leon Stein and
   Philip Taft.

Brooks, John Graham.
American Syndicalism. 1913.

Butler, Elizabeth Beardsley.
Women and the Trades. 1909.

Byington, Margaret Frances.
Homestead: The Household of A Mill Town. 1910.

Carroll, Mollie Ray.
Labor and Politics. 1923.

Coleman, McAlister.
Men and Coal. 1943.

Coleman, J. Walter.
The Molly Maguire Riots: Industrial Conflict in the Pennsylvania
    Coal Region. 1936.

Commons, John R.
Industrial Goodwill. 1919.

Commons, John R.
Industrial Government. 1921.

Dacus, Joseph A.
Annals of the Great Strikes. 1877.

Dealtry, William.
The Laborer: A Remedy for his Wrongs. 1869.

Douglas, Paul H., Curtis N. Hitchcock and Willard E. Atkins, editors.
The Worker in Modern Economic Society. 1923.

Eastman, Crystal.
Work Accidents and the Law. 1910.

Ely, Richard T.
The Labor Movement in America. 1890. New Introduction by
    Leon Stein and Philip Taft.

Feldman, Herman.
Problems in Labor Relations. 1937.

Fitch, John Andrew.
The Steel Worker. 1910.

Furniss, Edgar S. and Laurence Guild.
Labor Problems. 1925.

Gladden, Washington.
Working People and Their Employers. 1885.

Gompers, Samuel.
Labor and the Common Welfare. 1919.

Hardman, J. B. S., editor.
American Labor Dynamics. 1928.

Higgins, George G.
Voluntarism in Organized Labor, 1930-40. 1944.

Hiller, Ernest T.
The Strike. 1928.

Hollander, Jacob S. and George E. Barnett.
Studies in American Trade Unionism. 1906. New Introduction by
  Leon Stein and Philip Taft.

Jelley, Symmes M.
The Voice of Labor. 1888.

Jones, Mary.
Autobiography of Mother Jones. 1925.

Kelley, Florence.
Some Ethical Gains Through Legislation. 1905.

LaFollette, Robert M., editor.
The Making of America: Labor. 1906.

Lane, Winthrop D.
Civil War in West Virginia. 1921.

Lauck, W. Jett and Edgar Sydenstricker.
Conditions of Labor in American Industries. 1917.

Leiserson, William M.
Adjusting Immigrant and Industry. 1924.

Lescohier, Don D.
Knights of St. Crispin. 1910.

Levinson, Edward.
I Break Strikes. The Technique of Pearl L. Bergoff. 1935.

Lloyd, Henry Demarest.
Men, The Workers. Compiled by Anne Whithington and
  Caroline Stallbohen. 1909. New Introduction by Leon Stein
  and Philip Taft.

Lorwin, Louis (Louis Levine).
The Women's Garment Workers. 1924.

Markham, Edwin, Ben B. Lindsay and George Creel.
Children in Bondage. 1914.

Marot, Helen.
American Labor Unions. 1914.

Mason, Alpheus T.
Organized Labor and the Law. 1925.

Newcomb, Simon.
A Plain Man's Talk on the Labor Question. 1886. New Introduction
  by Leon Stein and Philip Taft.

Price, George Moses.
The Modern Factory: Safety, Sanitation and Welfare. 1914.

Randall, John Herman Jr.
Problem of Group Responsibility to Society. 1922.

Rubinow, I. M.
Social Insurance. 1913.

Saposs, David, editor.
Readings in Trade Unionism. 1926.

Slichter, Sumner H.
Union Policies and Industrial Management. 1941.

Socialist Publishing Society.
The Accused and the Accusers. 1887.

Stein, Leon and Philip Taft, editors.
The Pullman Strike. 1894-1913. New Introduction by the editors.

Stein, Leon and Philip Taft, editors.
Religion, Reform, and Revolution: Labor Panaceas in the Nineteenth
  Century. 1969. New Introduction by the editors.

Stein, Leon and Philip Taft, editors.
Wages, Hours, and Strikes: Labor Panaceas in the Twentieth Century.
  1969. New introduction by the editors.

Swinton, John.
A Momentous Question: The Respective Attitudes of Labor and Capital. 1895. New Introduction by Leon Stein and Philip Taft.

Tannenbaum, Frank.
The Labor Movement. 1921.

Tead, Ordway.
Instincts in Industry. 1918.

Vorse, Mary Heaton.
Labor's New Millions. 1938.

Witte, Edwin Emil.
The Government in Labor Disputes. 1932.

Wright, Carroll D.
The Working Girls of Boston. 1889.

Wyckoff, Veitrees J.
Wage Policies of Labor Organizations in a Period of Industrial Depression. 1926.

Yellen, Samuel.
American Labor Struggles. 1936.

SERIES II

Allen, Henry J.
The Party of the Third Part: The Story of the Kansas Industrial Relations Court. 1921. *Including* **The Kansas Court of Industrial Relations Law** (1920) by Samuel Gompers.

Baker, Ray Stannard.
The New Industrial Unrest. 1920.

Barnett, George E. & David A. McCabe.
Mediation, Investigation and Arbitration in Industrial Disputes. 1916.

Barns, William E., editor.
The Labor Problem. 1886.

Bing, Alexander M.
War-Time Strikes and Their Adjustment. 1921.

Brooks, Robert R. R.
When Labor Organizes. 1937.

Calkins, Clinch.
Spy Overhead: The Story of Industrial Espionage. 1937.

Cooke, Morris Llewellyn & Philip Murray.
Organized Labor and Production. 1940.

Creamer, Daniel & Charles W. Coulter.
Labor and the Shut-Down of the Amoskeag Textile Mills. 1939.

Glocker, Theodore W.
The Government of American Trade Unions. 1913.

Gompers, Samuel.
Labor and the Employer. 1920.

Grant, Luke.
The National Erectors' Association and the International Association of Bridge and Structural Ironworkers. 1915.

Haber, William.
Industrial Relations in the Building Industry. 1930.

Henry, Alice.
Women and the Labor Movement. 1923.

Herbst, Alma.
The Negro in the Slaughtering and Meat-Packing Industry in Chicago. 1932.

[Hicks, Obediah.]
Life of Richard F. Trevellick. 1896.

Hillquit, Morris, Samuel Gompers & Max J. Hayes.
The Double Edge of Labor's Sword: Discussion and Testimony on Socialism and Trade-Unionism Before the Commission on Industrial Relations. 1914. New Introduction by Leon Stein and Philip Taft.

Jensen, Vernon H.
Lumber and Labor. 1945.

Kampelman, Max M.
The Communist Party vs. the C.I.O. 1957.

Kingsbury, Susan M., editor.
Labor Laws and Their Enforcement. By Charles E. Persons,
  Mabel Parton, Mabelle Moses & Three "Fellows." 1911.

McCabe, David A.
The Standard Rate in American Trade Unions. 1912.

Mangold, George Benjamin.
Labor Argument in the American Protective Tariff Discussion.
  1908.

Millis, Harry A., editor.
How Collective Bargaining Works. 1942.

Montgomery, Royal E.
Industrial Relations in the Chicago Building Trades. 1927.

Oneal, James.
The Workers in American History. 3rd edition, 1912.

Palmer, Gladys L.
Union Tactics and Economic Change: A Case Study of Three
  Philadelphia Textile Unions. 1932.

Penny, Virginia.
How Women Can Make Money: Married or Single, In all Branches of
  the Arts and Sciences, Professions, Trades, Agricultural and Mechanical Pursuits. 1870. New Introduction by Leon Stein and Philip Taft.

Penny, Virginia.
Think and Act: A Series of Articles Pertaining to Men and Women,
  Work and Wages. 1869.

Pickering, John.
The Working Man's Political Economy. 1847.

Ryan, John A.
A Living Wage. 1906.

Savage, Marion Dutton.
Industrial Unionism in America. 1922.

Simkhovitch, Mary Kingsbury.
The City Worker's World in America. 1917.

Spero, Sterling Denhard.
The Labor Movement in a Government Industry: A Study of Employee Organization in the Postal Service. 1927.

Stein, Leon and Philip Taft, editors.
Labor Politics: Collected Pamphlets. 2 vols. 1836-1932. New Introduction by the editors.

Stein, Leon and Philip Taft, editors.
The Management of Workers: Selected Arguments. 1917-1956. New Introduction by the editors.

Stein, Leon and Philip Taft, editors.
Massacre at Ludlow: Four Reports. 1914-1915. New Introduction by the editors.

Stein, Leon and Philip Taft, editors.
Workers Speak: Self-Portraits. 1902-1906. New Introduction by the editors.

Stolberg, Benjamin.
The Story of the CIO. 1938.

Taylor, Paul S.
The Sailors' Union of the Pacific. 1923.

U.S. Commission on Industrial Relations.
Efficiency Systems and Labor. 1916. New Introduction by Leon Stein and Philip Taft.

Walker, Charles Rumford.
American City: A Rank-and-File History. 1937.

Walling, William English.
American Labor and American Democracy. 1926.

Williams, Whiting.
What's on the Worker's Mind: By One Who Put on Overalls to Find Out. 1920.

Wolman, Leo.
The Boycott in American Trade Unions. 1916.

Ziskind, David.
One Thousand Strikes of Government Employees. 1940.